KU-485-604

THE HIGHLANDS OF SCOTLAND

1 GLEN BRITTLE AND THE CUILLINS, ISLE OF SKYE

*From a Pastel Drawing
by W. Douglas Macleod*

THE HIGHLANDS
of SCOTLAND

By
HUGH QUIGLEY

Illustrated from Photographs by
ROBERT M. ADAM

NEW YORK
CHARLES SCRIBNER'S SONS
LONDON: B. T. BATSFORD LTD.
1936

First Published, March 1936

MADE AND PRINTED IN GREAT BRITAIN

TO

HUGH

In Memory of
Catacol and Aviemore

PREFACE

I HAVE made no effort to supply an all-embracing, all-descriptive guide-book to the Scottish Highlands: the publications and the journal of the Scottish Mountaineering Club have covered the ground so exhaustively that practically nothing remains to be done. I have avoided all folk-lorist collections and anecdotes : from Sir Walter Scott to Alexander Smith and H. V. Morton the literature is immense and easily accessible, and it is not essential, on the whole, to an appreciation of the Highland landscape and the Highland spirit. Place-name controversies—and they are legion—merely distract and confuse without enlightening, and potted history is always unsatisfactory. Travel books devoted to the Highlands have been so numerous in recent years—some wholly bad; some remarkably good, as Seton Gordon's *Highways and Byways in the Western Highlands*; some mere collections of itineraries; some interesting, if hackneyed, geographical, historical and purely literary pot-pourri;—that it would be sufficient to select a few of the best of them and look no further.

What then remains ?

The present book is an attempt to answer that question. It is a series of impressions of the finest parts of the Highlands seen with the appreciative eye of the ordinary cultured individual with some knowledge of artistic, literary, even economic and industrial backgrounds, with few traditions and few inherited prejudices.

It may not show the traveller how and where and when to climb a mountain, but it gives him some idea of what he will find when he arrives. It deals fully with less-known but very fine areas such as the Lower Grampians and Lewis, and touches very briefly on well-trodden and fashionable haunts such as the Trossachs and the Braes of Balquhidder—perhaps too briefly. It makes no attempt to schedule any mountains by number, location or size, and avoids with care the Highland towns such as Inverness, Perth or Oban, not because they are uninteresting in themselves, but because they are not sufficiently beautiful or original to merit a long journey for their own sake.

The book is, consequently, more a collection of high points or suggestions than of full-length descriptions; it indicates but seldom explores possibilities; its adventures are fireside adventures, arm-chair expeditions with the hint of vast spaces and infinite stretches of colour-filled air.

The wise man will dip into it and get his information from the guide-books, the folk-lorist annals or the place-names symposia (if he has a yearning for such things), buy a good one-inch map of the district selected, add to it a Bartholomew half-inch map to give the mountain masses clearly, since the new Ordnance Survey maps give the bare contour lines with no shading, or, if he is lucky, find an older version of the one-inch maps where such shading is given. (The four pages of maps given at the end of this volume, it may be explained, are included simply in the hope that they will prove useful for occasional reference during the course of reading, and are obviously inadequate—nor could they possibly be made adequate within these limits—to provide any form of basis for a planned tour.) He will rejoice in the special "Cairngorm" tourist map, but avoid the "Lower Strathspey" map as a snare and a delusion. He will browse through the *S.M.T. Journal* with persistency and read with care occasional and learned numbers of journals like the *Deeside Field*; or more wisely still brush aside this para-phernalia and take a chance on the hills himself. In them alone will he find his full and sufficient reward.

I have to thank Miss Cherkesi, Miss Ismay Goldie, Mr. E. W. Ashcroft, Mr. H. C. Hedderwick and Mr. E. G. Trent for the help they have given me in preparing and writing the book. My debt to Mr. Robert Adam is a considerable one, for it is his superb photography that completes the written descrip-tion and, perhaps more realistically than any words can do, conveys to the reader something of the magnificence of Highland landscape.

HUGH QUIGLEY.

Esher, *March* 1936.

CONTENTS

2   THE CLIMBER : Beneath the Cliffs of Cairn Lochan in the Cairngorms

3   EARLY SPRING IN THE HIGHLANDS : Glen Carron, Wester Ross

THE HIGHLANDS OF SCOTLAND

CHAPTER I

THE HIGHLANDS AND THE HIGHLAND SPIRIT

I REMEMBER as a boy standing in front of a picture by Colin Hunter in the Kelvingrove Art Galleries, admiring with wistfulness the blue hills and the sunset-coloured sea. The "Good-night to Skye" had the nostalgic quality which invests the whole of the Highland landscape. The beauty of hill and valley and moor has not the sharp-cut excellence of the Alps or even of the Lake District; it is finer and rarer and more appealing—something indefinable and yet penetrating, which has a suggestion beyond the capacity of the confidential poets and easy prose writers.

It is easy to become sentimental in the attempt to understand it. The more sympathetic may even have a sensation of repulsion and acute distaste, but no one can remain indifferent or detached. When one attempts, however, to obtain a perspective either in time or in place, one finds an extraordinary confusion of thought and of feeling—a jumble of associations, some of them romantic and all of them attractive. Should one attempt the Colin Hunter approach and become lost in a picture of immense landscapes shadowed by overarching clouds, great wastes of sea, edged at the skyline with the blue shadows of mountains, or should one push all this aside and look at the bare human reality beneath?

We may have a contempt for the conventions of a Landseer and deplore a civilisation modelled according to the best Balmoral traditions, but those Victorians saw something in the Highlands which had a powerful appeal for them. Their mental and spiritual make-up was not such as to give them acute appreciation of fine values, and they felt, obscurely perhaps, a little bit of the inspiration which gave beauty to the visions of a Hunter or a MacTaggart. They only lacked the capacity to abandon a hard, machine-made convention of admiration, all the harder because it was sanctified by Royalty. Only now, when we look at the efforts of a decayed

5   " THE ROUGH BOUNDS OF CORROUR " : Loch Ossian, in the Rannoch District, frozen over

surrounding them, although it might be diluted with clouds of an impalpable substance, had always the quality of a golden shimmer; the ethereal suggestion ardently, meticulously and patiently carried out by stock materials and methods made the Highlands an inferior kind of stage decoration, not crude enough for pantomime but good enough to be a judicious addition to a high-class Kensington interior. Cattle standing in their own reflection in calm lochs harmonised beautifully with old English Toby jugs and Chelsea shepherdesses.

A later school, imbued with Gothic or pseudo-Gothic ideals, saw in the mountains, not a gracious assemblage of harmonious and seductive forms, but the most brutal manifestations of the Gothic spirit. That school reached its lowest point of banality in the works of Landseer and in minor artists closely adhering to pre-Raphaelite conceptions.

Horatio McCulloch must be taken as the first artist to bring out the immensity of the Highland landscape. One can still admire his "Glencoe," "Loch Maree," "Glen Affric," "Loch Lomond," even though one may violently dislike his browns and muddy greens and opaque greys. The McCulloch tradition, which had much in common with that of Landseer, disappeared very soon in the early works of what is known as the Glasgow school of painting. It is this Glasgow school which has established the contemporary conception and appreciation of the Highland landscape.

One has only to think of the seascapes done by Mac-Taggart, particularly of "The Paps of Jura," and follow the glory of line and colour through later painters, such as the Hendersons and S. J. Peploe, to understand why the present generation finds such an attraction in the West Coast of Scotland. For MacTaggart and his contemporaries the atmosphere of the Highlands had a power of inspiration deeper than anything yet recorded in modern art.

When one moves from the sea into the mountains and from the mountains down into the moors, one sees the immense patterns vivid with brilliant colour of D. Y. Cameron or George Houston; one unconsciously simplifies, as Cameron simplified in his hills of Skye and his Arran; one draws iridescent colour, rich with a suggestion of autumn, over the green landscape winding through a fold in the hills, because that is how Houston and Strang and their school saw it and communicated their vision.

The force of this association still exerts the most powerful influence on the mind of the traveller in the Highlands. It has been strengthened in most recent times by the work of colourists such as Cecil Hunt, William Egginton, James Kay, James McBey, Robert Houston and James Patterson. Those artists see the Highlands as freshly as Cameron or Walton, but they lay stress more on atmosphere than on the weight of mountain and cliff.

Ben Nevis, in the hands of Cecil Hunt, turns a smooth grey back to a landscape drowned in the pale blue of the sky which lies over the mountain and over the moor at its foot. In Egginton's annual exhibition the sea is invariably in the distant lochs and the mountains are simplified to masses of colourful light and shade with few projections and few contortions. Hughes Stanton, a lover of Avignon, the Rhone Valley and Provence, transfers a difficult palette to the mountains of Mull, and one makes the amazing discovery that there is no real difference between a view of Mull from the top of Ben Mor and the Riviera from the Corniche Road. And Stanton is right, when the time and the weather coincide to give the landscape that magnificence of fine colour which is a quality of Southern France, and such occasions are probably more frequent in the West of Scotland than in the South of France.

In the last week of November 1935 a series of Highland landscapes by an artist unknown to me—a Mr. Joseph Gray —was sold at Messrs. Sothebys, landscapes of what ought to be well-known views of Lochnagar, the Cairngorms, Speyside and Loch Garry. In their ethereal aspect of tenuous blues and greens and purples and emeralds, reminiscent slightly of Copley Fielding, they showed to what slight memory of very beautiful things the Highland landscape could be reduced by a romantic mind.

Stress is laid on the visual interpretation because one of the joys of visiting a country like the Highlands lies in the comparison of vision taken at second-hand with the actual view of the original; the second-hand vision may help to give character and life to what might otherwise appear a very dull conglomeration of natural objects.

Or one might imagine what the Highlands were centuries ago when what are now bare hillsides were covered with magnificent forests which had their own influence on the climate. Those forests have disappeared long since, owing to lack of planning or conservation, leaving areas which are as big a problem in the Highlands as eroded areas in the

Tennessee Valley in the United States. When the trees go, and with them some of the vital things which make an area capable of cultivation, the process of deforestation, which is tantamount to denudation, continues uninterrupted.

The great clearance periods, which reached their highest point during the last war, can no longer be expected, but Deeside and the glens off the Caledonian Canal still echo to the sawmill, and the shower of pitprops and railway sleepers, although slight now, has never altogether ceased.

The face of the landscape changes without interruption, but even so the climate remains less hostile than one would expect. It is still true that the warmest areas of Great Britain are to be found on the West Coast. Frost is less frequent in the deeply indented inlets of the West Coast than it is in the extreme South of England. Palm trees grow easily in the gardens of the Kintyre Peninsula and the quality of the flowers in wind-protected gardens as far north as Ross and Cromarty can only be paralleled in carefully sheltered corners south of the Border. What the loss of the trees has done, however, has been to destroy much of the natural drainage of many areas, and so the marshes increase and fields which were once dry and fertile are now sour expanses of yielding bog, made beautiful only by the cotton grass, and the sides of the mountains rot away in the constant succession of rain-storms.

To bring the landscape, as a consequence, back to cultivation would require one of the greatest efforts of modern reclamation. Such a work might cause a new type of landscape to emerge altogether. One can hardly imagine the Wolf of Badenoch, as he struggled through the dense forests of Speyside, to be as conscious of the massif of the Cairngorms as we are now conscious of its immensity when we gaze at it across miles of open country.

Whether this type of landscape is one which is essential to the preservation of the Highland spirit, and with it the attraction of the Highlands, is a question that no one can easily answer. One could not feel any real regret at the closing in of perspective and the darkening of colour. The great clouds gloom in deep skies over shadowy mountains, held in a distance which has no limit—mountains with bare flanks open to glowing colours and purple shadows and the blue haze of the distance. The treeless landscape has taken from the air itself a superb attraction; one is now content merely to gaze at the marshes reflecting the clouds and the sunset without asking whether, under a wiser dispensation, those marshes might not have been large green fields multitudinous with cattle.

There are signs, however, that this period of contentment is coming to an end. The Forestry Commission has been active in many devastated areas, particularly in Speyside, and in the glens running east and west from the Caledonian Canal, planting wide stretches of new forest which may in time clothe the hillsides again. The complaint now is that the Commission has not been courageous enough to plan extensive areas of the Highlands or to push their planting programme high enough up the hillsides. It has also been accused of enclosing areas which might, with a little care, have been brought into good condition as arable or grazing land.

A further cause of criticism is the less obvious desire to make the areas under its control accessible to the public, due no doubt to an excessive preoccupation with old shooting and hunting rights.

Nevertheless, the Forestry Commission has at last put a check to a process lasting over several centuries and may be expected to effect a change in the face of Scotland.

One can already trace broad changes in the human or economic aspect of the Highlands. First of all, there were dense forests with a few clear areas cultivated eagerly by the dependents of the clan system; then the retreat of the forests and an increasing preponderance of cultivation; later the destruction of clan life, which enforced exile on the leaders of the communal life and surrendered whole regions to wild Nature; the triumph of the conception that sheep-farming is easier and more profitable than arable land or dairy-farming over extensive areas; the exhaustion of the sheep farms resulting from inability to understand the essentials of this type of farming and the completion of the surrender to Nature by the growth of the deer forests and the accompanying forcible removal of a great section of the farming population.

The deer-forest stage is now probably past—it is being rapidly destroyed by the changing taste of that section of the population which made this type of activity profitable in the past. Contemporary life is so full of diversions and distractions, many of them imposing all the mental and muscular strain of deer-shooting without any of its discomfort, that further indulgence in this sport has been rendered unnecessary and perhaps even undesirable.

6 A NORTHERN DEER-FOREST : Flowerdale, near Gairloch, Wester Ross

7. A CROFTING TOWNSHIP IN SKYE: Tarscavaig, on Loch Eishort, looking to the Cuillin Hills

The decay of the deer forest has coincided with, and is probably the result of, the disappearance of Balmoralism. It is becoming exceedingly difficult to let deer forests on a profitable basis, and so the deer-hunting lairds, with no real interest in the country and no stake in its prosperity, have carried their speculative activities elsewhere and the death-duties and similar taxation have added to the break-up of large estates. In many cases, in the Kintyre Peninsula, for example, this has not been a good thing. It removed from areas in danger of stupid commercial exploitation a restraining influence which has always worked for the preservation of beauty. In other areas, such as Glencoe and the glens off the Caledonian Canal, the break-up of those estates has led to the infusion of new blood determined to extract some economic benefit from what might have been described previously as devastated areas. So one comes slowly to the more modern phase—a phase brought about partly by the activities of the Forestry Commission. The opening up of the Highlands to interests other than those of deer-hunting lairds and restrictive hermits has coincided with the first attempt to bring back its original character to the Highland landscape.

The prostitution of the Highlands to the deer-hunting interests has not ended with the destruction of the old agricultural economy of the clans and the crofters, or with the destruction of the shielings and the small farms and the elimination of farmers and agricultural workers by forcible clearances; it has extended to communications as well—inns, hotels and guest-houses, necessities of travel from one point to another, have been kept down to the minimum.

One cannot accuse those interests of holding up road development, because such development is conditioned by the wealth or poverty of the counties responsible for roads, and the willingness or unwillingness of the Government to subsidise road construction. But one cannot doubt the fact that in a very large section of the Highlands, particularly in Inverness-shire, all the influence of the landlords has been used to prevent the construction of hotels and guest-houses, to obstruct the extension of existing hotels and to deter the traditional hospitality of the Highland people. In certain areas there is a veto on the right of any householder to give hospitality to a traveller, no matter what the weather conditions may be.

One has, therefore, a picture of deliberate organisation to

secure full value to speculation in deer forests. For many years the profits of such speculation were probably high enough to justify it, but it has been inimical to the real interests of the Highland people and the Highland landscape. One can imagine a country so split up into small holdings, that the right of the public to wander over it would be naturally circumscribed. That is the case in Italy and to some extent in the Tyrol. One can also imagine the country laid down to schemes of afforestation, water preservation and utilisation, where some check is necessary on movements of a travelling population. In those two cases one could hardly have any real objection. The country is performing a natural function. It is giving something to increase the wealth and happiness of its people. One can scarcely believe that a country where land is not cultivated, where afforestation is being developed in small sections sporadically, where the most determined resistance is being offered to any plan of water preservation and water development, was destined by nature to be so sterilised.

Sterility can have no real value, even for deer forest purposes. When, in addition, it is deliberate sterilising, where useless crop-heather is cultivated to provide food for useless game of practically no market value, one may begin to appreciate that special interests can go beyond sterilisation and bring the land to a point when it is incapable of recovery for agricultural or other purposes.

What, then, are the things which are permanently valuable in the Highland landscape? They are, first of all, human. We all know the stage Highlander acting as a ghillie for mock huntsmen sheltering behind butts on a stark mountain-side; the simple man who retails legends and myths of every loch and sticks a fairy tale on every peak; the dancer and the athlete who appears at the Highland games and makes a profession within a profession; the piper who can tune into the old lays of Scotland and give the warlike music of the clans. All those are part of the Victorian conception of a fit and proper Highland civilisation. What we do not know and cannot know is that type of Highlander who struggled to gain a reward out of the landscape, to wrest a living from difficult soil, to follow the highest standards of a culture dating from more than a thousand years back and to preserve full independence of spirit.

The Highlander at his highest level had the vision and the poetry of his Celtic ancestry. He had the qualities of loyalty,

8 NEW DWELLINGS FOR OLD: Isle of Barra, Outer Hebrides

9 SKERRAY, a typical Sutherland township on the north coast

10 AN ISLAND COMMUNITY : Easdale, on the Isle of Seil, in the Firth of Lorne, Argyllshire

determination and unflinching courage, before the feudal system introduced the clans at all. He had faith in the strength and the kindliness of Nature, which to anyone else must have appeared brutal and merciless. That type, with its pre-occupation with things of the spirit, its desire for education and for knowledge, should not be identified with the humble adherents of the clans. It should be identified with those individualists who are still striving to gain a living from the sea.

This type, however, has gone from the Highlands, and is now to be found only in isolated corners, fine representatives of a humanity which has the democracy of mental ability combined with the moral security of tradition.

To bring new prosperity to the Highlands some method must be found of bringing out and strengthening the old Highland spirit and leading it into closer contact with the new and excellent things modern science has been creating, and is still capable of creating, in ever greater measure. One must face the situation that the present-day Highlanders do not lend themselves easily to any revolutionary schemes which require qualities of determination and hard work. The average Highland town, such as one finds at Inveraray, Campbeltown or Inverness, where the influx of visitors has not been sufficient to change fundamentally the character of the population, is not a pleasant sight. It has no qualities of good planning, it is devoid of good architecture and social amenity. It has all the appearance of defeat, in the listlessness of the individual members of the population, in the repellent slums in which they live, as well as in their unwillingness to exercise any right of independent criticism against traditional obscurantism.

If one were to measure the contribution of the Highlands to creative art in religious buildings and memorials, communal dwellings or sculpture, painting and illuminated MSS., one would find some difficulty in discovering anything of real value, but lack of such evidence is not enough proof of the inability of the Highland spirit to produce things of great beauty. There is the evidence of the Highland literature and, in modern times, of the small local industries of weaving, wood-working and carpet-making. In those things, the love of simple but good design and of lovely, if sometimes subdued, colour, blends in the appreciation of fine music to a depth of emotional expression such as does not exist anywhere else. And so one comes to the conclusion, willingly, that the typical Highland town is not representative of what the

c

Highland mind could do if it had full liberty of creation, liberty to draw inspiration from the hills and the clouds and the blue seas. The effort must be made to find that liberty and bring it back into the soul of the people.

At the present time, the traveller in the Highlands, alienated and offended by temporary structures built of corrugated iron, is inclined to look on the Highlands as examples of corrugated-iron civilisation, forgetful of the poverty of the people and of their inability to restore wealth to a devastated landscape. After all, those repellent little villages are no more hateful than the colonies which are scattered broadcast over the Southern England counties, in Hampshire and Devon; they could never be as bad as the new seaside resorts built by jazz architects in the vicinity of Clacton-on-Sea. One does miss the simplicity of good architectural planning, and this feeling of loss is not made good by the appreciation of little towns and villages which are good examples of traditional and communal architectural beauty. The Campbeltowns and Inverarays and Invernesses, with an occasional building to relieve their drabness and their grey misery, are little better than slums, but Speyside provides some choice examples of perfect communal centres. Kingussie and Grantown-on-Spey are peaceful, stone-built, simply-designed towns, especially Grantown with its great square arranged round a tree-shadowed green, and if we go farther south there is another good example in Pitlochry. The Highlands cannot be regarded as incapable of producing fine things when there is some opportunity to do so, and with some guidance, their contribution to the arts could be immensely increased. On the human side, therefore, the Highlands are not entirely hopeless.

On the economic and industrial sides the prospects of the revival are good, if not immediately productive. In the early years, traditional deer-hunting interests put up the most determined resistance to water-power development, and it is only now that this resistance has tended to disappear.

One could find here some reason for objection. Industrialism, as far as it has touched the Highlands, has not been a beautiful or an admirable thing. Fort William, as a new industrial town, is in the grand old tradition of Scottish industrialism, ugliness and squalor, widely distributed poverty with no indication of anything higher than the mere process of making money, and Kinlochleven still leaves much to be desired. Neither has the type of labour employed in carrying out the large water-power schemes in those hills been such as to

11 GRANTOWN-ON-SPEY : A Highland country town, " peaceful, stone-built, simply designed "

12   THE SHORES OF LOCH RANNOCH, PERTHSHIRE

disarm suspicion. The colonising of the Highlands by the type of low-grade Irishman, which has reduced Clydeside to a sub-civilised area, cannot be regarded as an improvement on the ghillies and retainers used by the deer-hunting interests to keep the landscape devoid of human life.

One could find, therefore, some justification for the opposition put up by Highland interests to the extension of the Fort William tradition, even if one might be inclined to suspect the sincerity and the credentials of those lovers of the amenities. There is to-day a new perception at work regarding the use of water-power resources. Such resources, if applied merely to the manufacture of aluminium, have not the same social and economic value as when used to facilitate the economic development of the whole area. The Grampian scheme, one of the largest of its kind in Europe, has been carried out with sufficient care of the amenities, particularly in the construction of dams, runways and power stations, to ensure that those developments should not conflict with the landscape itself. The best evidence of this is a film prepared by Paul Rotha and entitled *The Face of Britain,* which would have been more accurately called " The Face of the Scottish Highlands and Industrial England."

The Grampian scheme uses up the resources of the area round the Moor of Rannoch and of the lochs feeding into the river Tummel and into Loch Rannoch itself, so that this desolate area which forms so thrilling a chapter in *Kidnapped* is beginning to wear the trappings of civilisation, contemporary machine civilisation, with the clean lines and sharp, simple masses of monolithic concrete construction which, even to the casual view, have an intimate association with the great cliffs and corries surrounding them. The purist, looking at Schiehallion across the transparent waters of Loch Rannoch, may turn round and gaze with amazement and perhaps repulsion at the line of the towers gliding over the moors, and proclaim aloud the desecration of the landscape. But is it desecration? Is it not rather the first clear sign of new life which will change the landscape so radically that it will no longer be an uninhabited sterile wilderness but a rich country, alive and happy with human activity. The difference between the great aluminium schemes and the Grampian scheme lies precisely in the fact that the latter is bringing a new amenity and a new source of power into every single remaining activity in the Highlands. It makes no distinction of time, nor of place, nor of occupation. It is inhuman and impartial, but it thrives on the measure of its service; it cannot live in seclusion or lend itself to discrimination. It is a universally active force which depends for its wealth-earning power on the speed with which it is universally applied. One can see now the ancient land of Badenoch, the home of the earliest Scottish clan, traversed by the towers and poles carrying this new force, and if to that force is added determination to bring back the old agricultural economy and to strengthen it by everything modern science can contribute, then one may in the process of years see an even more rapid process of revival.

Appreciation of this possibility has been slow to enter the Highland mind, but of recent years conversion has been so rapid that expectancy may so far exceed results as to breed despondency.

To-day the Wade policy of road-making has been changed to something more valuable. Wade built his roads in a purely militarist sense. He desired to make it easy for the legions of modern Rome to penetrate into the inaccessible wastes of the Highlands and win tatterdemalion victories. He arranged for garrisons to be located at new forts, Fort Augustus, Fort William and at Kingussie, for the purpose of keeping the Highlands in subjection and with no intention of developing the new road systems into anything more valuable than channels for oppression. It is doubtful whether the clansmen at that time would have been amenable to any plan of "colonial" development, and it is probably only now that the change in mentality and in the approach to the fundamental things of life has been sufficiently great to permit of conversion. The resistance to the water-power schemes as recently as 1926 shows some relics of this old spirit of noncompromise and conservative reaction.

The Wade tradition has now been supplanted by a new and better policy which may in time enshrine a noble tradition. Road-making in the Highlands has attained such proportions as to change the character of the landscape. Two main arteries have been built to link up the Highlands with the main centres of population farther south. The Great North Road runs uncompromisingly over the Central Highlands, through Badenoch and up Speyside to Inverness. To the west of the Great North Road, the other artery links up Fort William with the Scottish Lowlands on the one side and with Inverness on the other. The new road up the Great Glen was brought to a conclusion early in 1935, and is probably one of the most important feats of road engineering in this country; it must become the backbone of a whole series of lateral roads debouching on the Great Glen. Under a new dispensation, the main arteries will feed into new roads opening up difficult areas of Inverness, Banffshire and Aberdeenshire. They may be extended in time to reach Ross and Cromarty and Sutherlandshire.

Here, again, the lover of the old desolate amenities may deplore the intrusion of a motor civilisation and object to the silence of the glens being destroyed by the raucous clamour of mechanical transport, but the Highlands can absorb this type of activity with ease. They are so imposing in their magnificence that the most spectacular and noisy of human activities is as nothing beside them. They did not flinch before the enormities of corrugated iron steadings and hamlets or the blank concrete masses of the water-power works. Their beauty survived the influence of the ghastly monastery built at Fort Augustus which summarises the dreariness and monotony of that uninteresting little town.

It is possible to exaggerate the decline of Scotland and particularly of the Highlands. The Census indicates a very rapid decline in population, with no apparent signs of coming to an end, but it is legitimate to ask a question: would it be possible to put a population into the Highlands as great as that which lived at the highest point of development in the past, notably towards the end of the seventeenth and the beginning of the eighteenth centuries? The standard of living in Scotland at that period was already so low and the poverty so extreme that the country could maintain a large population without serious further economic stress, and there is a sufficiency of evidence to prove that the hardship and depression was as notable a characteristic of Scottish economy then as now. The contemporary standards of living may make it desirable to be content with a small population and bring within its reach a wider range of products. There is a telling chapter in a publication of Robert Woodrow, entitled *Memoirs of Reformers and Ministers of the Church of Scotland*, which gives a contemporary account of Scotland in 1724:

"There is a profound peace at present, and nothing stirring of any publick nature almost, Things are in suspense abroad, and, though our parties are warm enough in privat, and the humor great, yet there is little appearing in publick. Under this peace we are growing much worse. The gentry and nobility are generally either discontent, or Jacobite, or profane; and the people are turning loose, worldly and very disaffected. The poverty and debts of many are increasing, and I cannot see how it can be otherwise. Ther are no ways to bring in specie into this country. Trade is much failed, and any trade we have is of that kind that takes money from amongst us, and brings in French brandy, Irish meal, tea, etc., which are all consumed; and unless it be a feu coals from the West, and some black cattell from the South, and many of these are not our breed, but Irish, I see no branch of our business that brings in any money. Our tobacco trade, and other branches to the West Indies, are much sinking; and the prodigiouse run of our nobility and gentry to England, their wintering there, and educating their children there . . . takes away a vast deal of monney every year. Besides, its plain that we are overstocked with people, considering their idlness, and that makes the consumpt very great. . . . To say nothing of the vast losses many have susteaned by the South Sea and York Building, our oun Fishing Company, which, wer people faithfull, might bring in a great deal, and other bubles."

What is then at issue is not so much restoration of a prosperity which never really existed as the application of modern methods and modern knowledge to the old agricultural economy of the Highlands, with a view to ensure that it affords a greater measure of wealth than in previous centuries.

It may be unnecessary in a book of travel mainly devoted to description to dwell on this aspect of the Highlands, but even the most casual traveller might well know that one of the greatest issues of the future is going to be the resurrection of the Highlands, a resurrection based on an understanding of what the landscape can offer. It may, as a result of the development of water-power resources and the extension of transport facilities, take the form of a well-controlled tourist industry with all its apparatus of good transport services and good hotels; or of improved marketing, of fishing products especially, as an extension of the work carried out by the Argyll Fisheries. Or possibly it may take the form of deliberate expansion of small home industries, some indication of which is given by the weavers of the Hebrides in making the name "Harris Tweed" a trade-mark. It may be carried out by a more intelligent and enlightened programme of electro-chemical or electro-metallurgical development based

13 A WEST HIGHLAND STRONGHOLD: Castle Tioram on Loch Moidart, Argyllshire

14 LOOKING ACROSS LOCH LINNHE TO THE ARDGOUR HILLS

on water-power, and it may, in the last and most interesting phase, rely on the scientific exploitation of the forests of Scotland now being grown by the Forestry Commission.

There is already some impatience with the standards of service which have hitherto been accepted without complaint. The steamship services round the West Coast beyond the Firth of Clyde are still primitive enough to be romantic, but the contemporary spirit is not so fond of romance when it is associated with inconvenience and dirt as the hardier mid-Victorian. Even on a cattle steamer it likes to see some appreciation of modern design and modern convenience, and it will not be content much longer to be battered and tossed in ancient freighters which have casually become passenger-carrying steamers. The steamship companies have shown themselves receptive to this change in public opinion, but there is still an immense opportunity for improving sea communications on the West Coast of Scotland.

A similar observation applies to the railways. There is no real improvement in the railway communications in the Highlands, despite the glorification of new golf courses and amusement centres of the Gleneagles category, or spectacular trains for the opening of grouse shooting. One can dispense with such trains and expensive golf courses in favour of better ordinary rolling stock and service. The obvious remedy lies in the application of water-power to traction. The Highland Railway Company should have been the first to adopt electrification from water-power plants, and it will never give satisfactory service until it does so.

The sceptical may argue that there is little opportunity for really large changes either in Highland topography or Highland economy, but the influx of travellers into the country is already so great that it gives some idea of expansion to come, not far short of that which took place in Switzerland when "tourisme" became a national industry.

The poetical sampler of curiosities and the devotee of desolate spaces may lament the humanising of the Highlands, but it is a landscape which gains from human association. Even if one were to drive an arterial road through the Lairig Ghru, a plan sacrilegious in the extreme, the mountains would come closer, but in that proximity they would assume a more threatening poise.

The Highlands can become the greatest playground in Europe; they are already vested with the glamour of association with great historical movements of the past.

Free from unintelligent exploitation and brought into intimate contact with contemporary life, they can be a supremely happy region, vivid with human activity yet remote under the sky which is for ever changing in form and colour. We give to that landscape a nostalgic longing and take from it a nobler understanding of the meaning of life.

15 IN GLEN MORISTON WESTER ROSS

16 A GLADE ON THE RIVER RUEL, IN THE COWAL DISTRICT
OF ARGYLL

17   THE STEEP CLIFFS OF CAIRN LOCHAN, IN THE CAIRNGORMS

CHAPTER II

THE CAIRNGORMS

THE Cairngorms are hardly a part of the Scottish Highlands. They are a self-contained world of their own set in the middle of a frame of pastoral country, ripe in the wealth of its cultivation and its quiet, full beauty. Pedantry would confine the geographical definition of the Cairngorms to the groups north of Deeside and east of Speyside, but they should really include Lochnagar and the rolling hills which slope up from County Angus and culminate in Loch Callater west of Braemar and Dinnet Moor east of Braemar.

This mountainous country has all the qualities of the Scottish scene. It is the wildest and the most peaceful part of Scotland, and the background of the most romantic events in Scottish history and of some of the most sordid. On Deeside, it has been the field of the struggles of the clans, but in the Cairngorm massif itself feudal combats and relationships meant very little beside the power and desolation of the landscape. The attempt to introduce a literary quality into the Cairngorms and to vest them with fantastic and awe-inspiring legends or with an element of pathos, of the futility of humanity against the savagery and bleakness of Nature is fatal to their real appreciation. They do not require emotional interpretation nor sentimental camouflage. They must be accepted as they are, without compromise. However mellow and kind they may appear, hardly a season goes by without a disaster occurring in a deep glen or corrie or on the hilltop exposed to all the winds and fury of the sky. If one should, however, wander into the Cairngorms on an early spring or autumn day, one can scarcely credit such disasters, so easy are the approaches to the mountains and the slopes so gradual. While there are terrific precipices and corries, littered with ruin on the north-east face, the grading of Braeriach and of Ben Macdhui down to the pass at the summit of the Lairig Ghru is as regular as if it had been smoothed out by a machine, and the destructive processes of time have tended to remove excrescences and wear down projections until the ingenuous visitor comments on the immense humps of rock and scorns their slopes. Yet their attraction lies possibly in this combination of easy approach and difficult physical conditions. One can reach any top, with the exception possibly of Cairntoul, without serious difficulty, but on the top there is no protection against storm or rain, and the distances even on the flat are a test of endurance.

The mountains form an island projecting into an extensive plain, so that one has an impression of walking along the edge of the world, Scotland stretching out into the far distance beneath.

Of all the mountains of Scotland which call for slow and sure appreciation, the Cairngorms come first. They lend themselves to distant perspectives which give them the value of their bulk. Taken together, their lack of outstanding features makes them appear less impressive; the symmetrical pointed peaks of the smaller mountains guarding the approach to the Lairig Ghru, and of Cairntoul, are not silhouetted sharply against the sky as isolated mountains are in Sutherland, but form almost an uninterrupted frieze of colour across the horizon.

One has only to stand on the railway station at Aviemore in the early light of a grey morning and look across to the Cairngorms as they stretch behind Rothiemurchus to see how harmoniously every block, cliff, shoulder, scar and peak fits into the solid mountain mass and yet retains individuality of colour, of shadow and light, and know what is the most moving character of the Cairngorms. They lie in a band of pure colour, colour changing to colour at every moment. In the late afternoon, when the cumulus rolls over them, they disappear so completely into their background that one cannot tell where a cloud ends and a hill begins. One can go over the brook to the golf course stretched at the foot of Craigellachie and spend a whole day watching the changing patterns which are woven over the hills by the sky and the clouds. And the texture changes as much as the colour and the shape; the clouds sweep up in an everlasting flood from the Lairig Ghru, rest on the Cairn Lochan, then roll away to be balanced on a single point of Cairngorm. They come in a solid mass to Braeriach, spread to Ord Ban and to the forests round Loch an Eilein, until only the nearer hills, west of

18   THE SNOW-CLAD CAIRNGORMS, seen from Glen More across Loch Morlich

19 REFLECTIONS IN ROTHIEMURCHUS FOREST, STRATHSPEY

20 THE GREAT CORRIE, BEINN A' BHUIRD, IN THE CAIRNGORMS

Loch Morlich, emerge, sharp and distinct in the intensity of colour.

There is no halt in this play of cloud and land, and even on a cloudless day, when the sky is a shimmering blue overhead, the peaks are etched out in exquisite line and the corries lie in a deep haze. The opening of the pass disappears then behind the old trees of Rothiemurchus Forest, and as the sun rises higher the haze advances more and more until the mountains are a trembling presence shadowed vaguely across the bottom of the sky.

At night, when the haze is gone, the hills rush forward to the eyes, bitter and gloomy, and the Cairngorms become once more the threatening visions of the Celtic mind.

From the terrace of the great hotel one can watch sunsets so tumultuous and so extravagant in colour that no painter could reproduce them without being accused of crudeness or sensationalism. At other times, when the sun is hidden, the landscape sighs out in a tenuous grey light which has no definition.

Yet with all this multitudinous and changeable magnificence, the impression of majesty is seldom present. One has to move deeper into Nairn and the northern plains to get some idea of the immensity of the Cairngorms. At Grantown-on-Spey, where the corries of the Cairngorm are visible and the Bynacks lie abruptly at the beginning of the Lairig an Laiogh, one can get a measure of their vastness without experiencing any other emotion than that evoked by fine line and clear atmosphere. But in the flat country south of Nairn, the world becomes smoothed out to an insignificant pattern of fields overshadowed by the immense mountain mass blocking up the sky. The only other mountain which has this quality of becoming impressive with distance is Ben Nevis.

On the southern side at Braemar there is no perspective, as there are no plains; and the mountain groups are so tightly massed together and the valleys so narrowed down that the highest peaks are only curved shoulder above curved shoulder: so much so that one must have a nice taste in shoulders to make any distinction between them. Even here one can place the Cairngorms in perspective by going up a flat valley to Loch Callater. If one looks back after some miles, Cairntoul emerges in a single self-contained picture, balanced with perfect symmetry on a series of rising waves of mountains. Or one can go along the Dee almost as far as Invercauld

Bridge and see the high corries of Beinn a' Bhuird, white on the edge of a purple curtain held up on either side by the high larches and reflected in the calm waters of the river.

The Cairngorms are, on the whole, dry mountains. They have, like any other mountain range, wet sides and dry sides, but the steepness of the slopes and the stony character of the river beds leads the water away fairly rapidly and keeps the footpaths, where they exist, reasonably dry.

The approaches to the mountains, although they cover many miles of desolate moor, are not made difficult by bogs such as one meets in the Isle of Arran, although the moors just before the Ryvoan Pass are sticky; the Deeside half of the Lairig Ghru walk, for the first five or six miles at least, is practically a continuous swish through running water and the narrow footpath from the White Mount down to Loch Callater is slimy and slippery in parts.

On the whole, however, the Cairngorms, if we exclude the Monadliath Mountains on the west bank of the river Spey, are not difficult to climb. What they call for is physical endurance to cover very long distances. To reach the top of Cairngorm, for example, one must cover a distance of over seven miles on the flat from Aviemore, and before the ascent has been completed and the traveller returns to his hotel, a distance of about twenty-five miles will have been covered.

The most comprehensive picture of the Cairngorm range is gained by going about a mile and a half south of Aviemore to Easter Lynwilg and proceeding up the glen to the right, along a road which leads ultimately to the river Dulnan, and along the Dulnan back into Speyside. A little over a mile up this path, just beyond the wood, one comes out on the first buttress of the clumsy-looking mountain called Geal-charn Mor. One need only climb on to the first ridge of this buttress to enjoy one of the finest panoramas in Britain.

Loch Alvie lies beneath in its frame of woods, its calmness stirred by a passing wind, and Loch Insh lies away to the south, a thin silver streak between the pines. Beyond them the Spey is invisible except when it sweeps into open meadows beyond Kinrara and curves back again into shadow beyond Aviemore. To the east of this valley, held together by the two lochs, a broad plateau opens out to vivid green pastures or to clusters of birches. Behind this plateau rise the Cairngorms, range behind range, valley grading into valley, until the sweep round to Craiggowrie closes the perspective to the north beyond Glenmore Forest.

The most striking part of the landscape is not the high peaks of the Cairngorms, seen here in all their breadth and splendour over the clouds, but in the harmony of complicated curves of Sgoran Dubh Mor, and its highest peak Sgor Gaoith, which glooms above the black waters of Loch Einich, more than 2000 feet below.

This block of mountains throws out a series of buttresses down into thickly wooded Glen Feshie, overshadowing the lower hills which lie to the south-west beyond Loch An t-Seilich and the strange, wild Gaick country, a land of dread to the superstitious Gael. This whole country round Glen Feshie is not so favourite a centre, but it has its own power to inspire admiration and even humility.

When the upper plateau had been reached on the shoulders and buttresses of the Sgoran Dubh Mor group, which is as green as a lawn in the height of summer, one could gallop on horseback for miles. And the walk from Creag Dhubh along the narrow ridge to Sgoran Dubh Mor, with views of Glen Einich and of the gloomy crescent of rock which closes it in the south, up by easy stages, over an ever-broadening upland country, until one reaches a final peak which appears almost to overhang Glen Feshie, is one of the most remarkable experiences in Scotland. This is no spectacular hill-climbing but easy going on turf, dry under foot.

Badenoch and Speyside have still memories of great characters and great occasions. More than a century ago, Sir Thomas Dick Lauder described, in a novel conceived in the pure Scott tradition, the character and adventures of a turbulent mediæval chieftain, Alexander Stuart, the son of King Robert the Second, Earl of Buchan, Earl of Ross, Lord of Badenoch, but known better as the Wolf of Badenoch. Stuart appears to have been rather a sordid and sorry villain, no matter how magnificent the decoration applied to him by the novelist; he ruled Badenoch and Speyside with a brutality and unscrupulousness which still makes him an object of horror tempered with admiration. From his castle on Loch an Eilein he dominated the whole of Speyside and defied the Bishop of Moray, whose cathedral he burned at Elgin in 1390.

The native Celtic inhabitants of this district and of the whole of Inverness, from sea to sea, right down to Braemar and west of Lochaber, belonged to Clan Chattan; the clan is described in the *Fair Maid of Perth*, where the struggle between them and Clan Kay at the North Inch of Perth, about the end of the fourteenth century, gave them some historical significance. The chiefs of Clan Chattan were Macintoshes, but they owed allegiance to landlords appointed by the Crown, such as the Earls of Huntly and Moray. The vicissitudes of such swashbuckling bullies as the Wolf of Badenoch were, however, foreign to the occupations of the people themselves. The clansmen, as far as they had any genuine loyalty, obeyed the local chieftains and generally found themselves in opposition to the foreign landlord imposed on them.

During the two centuries, from 1400 to 1600, when Clan Chattan held well together, it was represented by something like sixteen clans, the principals, other than the Macintoshes, who were supreme, being the MacPhersons and the Farquharsons. Up to the time of the second Jacobite Rebellion, the Macintoshes, with the Grants, MacPhersons and Farquharsons, were the clans principally in power in the Cairngorm region. They were not, on the whole, hostile to the Duke of Argyll and the Campbells; they preferred, as the history of the Montrose and Dundee campaigns, as well as the Jacobite Rebellion, show, to remain neutral, with a marked inclination to support the authority in power, and to that extent they found themselves at odds with the MacDonalds, who occupied the country farther west, especially the bellicose MacDonalds of Glengarry.

The history of the relationships of the clans, their innumerable struggles and internecine battles, is so complicated that it would require a mathematical genius to disentangle it, but even to this day, the tradition holds good in Speyside.

The campaigns of Montrose, described elsewhere, are the great occasions in the history of Speyside; the whole country owes its place in literature, other than purely Celtic, to MacPherson of Ossian, who was a native of Badenoch, and who set the fashion which was carried on by poets like John Clarke.

On the Braemar side, Queen Victoria and her school introduced a literary movement, the best title for which is "Balmoralism." Robert Louis Stevenson wrote *Treasure Island* in a small retired boarding-house at Braemar, and probably found in the atmosphere of the Cairngorms inspiration for some of the books which followed *Treasure Island*.

The district, if we are to judge from its place names, was known to the early Celtic saints, and this is not surprising because Speyside is the main highway to the north, and is

21   THE SWEEPING LINES OF THE GAIRN VALLEY, seen from Ben Avon, East Cairngorms

22   THE MASSIVE CLIFFS ABOVE LOCH AVON, IN THE CAIRNGORMS

23   LOCH AVON AND BEN MACDHUI, IN THE CAIRNGORMS

easily reached from the Great Glen by the road which passes the source of the Spey, or from the rich meadows of Perthshire through the river Garry at Dalwhinnie.

A rich store of literature or of religious and historical lore may not be essential to enjoyment of the Cairngorms, but it is interesting to remember that this country is one of the most ancient parts of Britain geologically and has associations deep in the story of humanity, and to know that many centuries ago the clans which populated it lived a semi-nomadic life in badly built and badly protected bothies and drove their cattle to and from the pastures on the plateau above. Occasionally, forgetting the teachings of the saints, the wild men of the glens would indulge their natural propensities and penetrate the Lairig Ghru, down to Braemar and from Braemar past Loch Callater, or through the pass of Ballater, down into the rich lowlands of Angus, and take their toll of the lowlanders' cattle. They came sometimes from Nethy Bridge *via* Lairig an Laoigh; at others they descended into Deeside *via* Tomintoul. The Cairngorms, storm-ridden and trying to the endurance of man and beast, have ever been a difficult barrier.

The mountaineering guide-books give a full description of the paths to be followed to reach the giants of the Cairngorms; less usual is the walk over the long plateau of the Sgoran Dubh Mor and the semicircular traverse of Beinn a' Bhuird and Ben Avon from Braemar past Glen Slugain. Those two groups are sufficiently isolated from the main mass to yield a rich reward of colour and perspective. The other groups, Braeriach and Cairntoul on the west side of the Lairig Ghru and Cairngorm, Ben Macdhui and Derry Cairngorm on the east side, are much more deeply enclosed and more unapproachable.

The wise man may find his pleasure in wandering over what remains of the Rothiemurchus and Glenmore Forests, without attempting to do more than climb up a small eminence to confirm the view. He could struggle up the steep, denscly-wooded hill which hides Loch an Eilein or Ord Ban, and get his fill of the magnificent landscape.

He could wander over the Spey Bridge, between the high larches and the pines as far as Coylumbridge and stumble patiently over the bumpy road leading to one of the finest lochs in the whole of the Highlands, Loch Morlich, and spend a happy summer afternoon bathing in its cool waters from its crescent of red-golden sand.

He could, if he were more energetic, walk through the forest along the footpath running north-west to meet the road from the Lairig Ghru, cross the Druie, rise out of the wood beside the lonely steading of Tullochgrue and see in the blue distance the valley of the Spey, with the curves of the rolling grey mountains shaped against the sky.

Or he might be content to struggle up the Ryvoan Pass, along the marshy moors into the Forest of Abernethy.

There are occasions, however, when the quality of the air is so fine that indulgence in easy things seems to be repellent. And so, one morning, with all the weather auspices on one's side, one slips out of the hotel at Aviemore and embarks on a first trial of strength.

The day I climbed up to the top of Braeriach I had every hope that the weather would be a perfect accompaniment. The night had been full of stars and there were no clouds in the early morning sky, so that the first five miles through Rothiemurchus, along the path to the right of the track which leads to the Lairig Ghru and up the easy slopes of Glen Einich, were filled with a well compounded pleasure. But soon the clouds came steeply over the slopes of Carn Eilrig and drifted in wisps and tatters and, occasionally, streamers, across the broken plateaux of the glen.

When I reached the first bothy, beside the first loch in the Glen—a marshy confusion of waters—I was debating in my mind whether I should take the immediate route to the top of Braeriach, up the river to the east of the bothy and round the steep edge of the corrie overlooking a wild little loch, when the rain came down in a solid mass and I could not face the prospect of wading through wet heather, three feet high. A party of gypsies was occupying the bothy, and a smoking chimney had its own attraction compared with the driving wind. But when I got half-way to the upper bothy, up a flat valley bottom, broken up by slow streams and immense boulders left behind by the glaciers, the sun came out again, pushing aside the mist and giving a first view of the formidable cliffs of Sgoran Dubh Mor. The loch beneath had not a particle of light in it: a solid black pavement with a narrow frill of white at the edge where it emptied into the river.

Beyond the second bothy, a path moved steeply upwards until it entered a smooth corrie, Coire Dhondail, giving a still more impressive view of the loch and of the cliffs which came round it in gloomy precipices, torn and broken under

24 GLEN EINICH, LOOKING TO BRAERIACH, IN THE CAIRNGORMS

25 LOCH EINICH, WITH THE SPUR OF SGORAN DUBH,
IN THE CAIRNGORMS

26   THE CLEFT OF SLOCHD MOR, LOOKING TOWARDS GLEN AVON, IN THE CAIRNGORMS

the light of the rainstorm. The corrie itself was not difficult, although the path went over steep slabs as it mounted to the upper plateau, and the last struggle up to the Einich Cairn and the Wells of Dee was difficult only because it came at the end of the climb and because the path lay over terraces of gravel alternating with stretches of sparse vegetation. At the Einich Cairn the day subsided altogether, the mists came down, the rain changed to snow, then to hail, and the task of sheltering in a wilderness which has no rocks or caves was one which would have daunted the most courageous.

For a few seconds the mist lifted and gave a remarkable view over the Garbh Choire down into the Lairig and along Deeside, across the lower slopes of Ben Macdhui. That ended the day's expedition because the weather made it impossible to go to the highest point of Braeriach, along the ridge to Sron na Lairig and thence down to Rothiemurchus past the sentinel hill of Carn Eilrig. A dreary and almost a murderous day, it left behind it a finer impression than the second time when, in fine weather and a blazing sun, I completed the pilgrimage.

In a mood of little determination one could wander up the slopes of Cairngorm, along a well-marked road, Loch Morlich growing smaller in the distance and the plain behind the Nethybridge moving slowly into vision and come, beyond the top of Cairngorm, upon perhaps the most inspiring corner of the whole range. Down the easy slopes, beneath the lip of the summit and beyond the boulders, lies a stretch of pasture land, with a small eminence rising to the right of it. How pleasant to walk down to that pasture, by Garbh Allt and Strathnethy and thence back to Glenmore . . . but without any warning the mild pasture land disappears abruptly in a sheer precipice, with a deep silent loch lying at the bottom of a drop of about a thousand feet, only the distant echo of a waterfall coming down into it across the Shelter Stone Crag—Loch Avon. The fiercest wind can scarcely move it into waves, and the sun at midday is little more than an attenuated glimmer. It is the loneliest loch in Scotland, with perhaps the most impressive single mountain view, with Loch Etchachan above, the snowcap of Ben Macdhui rising on the right and Derry Cairngorm straight in front.

One can go round Corrie Raibeirt to the Shelter Stone, spend a night there, and in the early morning wander down through the gloomy quiet of the precipices to the lochside

E

and thence to the Lairig an Laoigh, or follow the wild country
of the Avon to Inchrory and Tomintoul. Or strike farther
up the hillside, move round to Ben Macdhui, skirting the
cliffs of the Coire Sputan Dearg, cross the shoulder of Derry
Cairngorm down to the Derry Burn and thence to Braemar.

If unwilling to rest at the Shelter Stone, not content with the
first grand view down horizontal masses of cliff, one may
attempt the difficult passage along the east face of Cairngorm.
The going here is very difficult as masses of debris lie in the
path, so that the climber may be glad to leave the path,
struggle up beyond it to the Cnap Coire na Spreidhe and
down one of the steep buttresses of the Cairngorm to an
imaginary footpath, existing only on the map, over dreary
and difficult stretches of heather, swamp, shrub and sharp
projections of stone, down to a confusion of fences, most
of them impassable, until at last, in deep thankfulness, he
fords the stream and comes to the shores of calm and un-
utterably cruel Loch Morlich.

There is pleasure to be found in climbing Craigellachie,
through the birchwoods behind the racecourse and tracing
an arduous way past the little lochs which lie between it and
the first slopes of Carn Dearg Mor; thence over desolate and
boggy moorland beyond over the top and which lies a lonely
repellent-looking country with no outstanding features.
Here one can diverge to the right over a tussocky marsh
beside the Milton Burn, down through the woods again to
the sawmills at Eastern Aviemore, a picturesque group, and
thence back on to the main road.

This little expedition is no less remarkable than more
spectacular adventure in the high peaks of the Cairngorms,
because the landscape here has that quality of hopelessness
and dreariness which one associates with an imaginary
inferno. The only relief is an immense wood with uncertain
paths streaking through it; but beauty here is only half
revealed.

The three expeditions which *must* be undertaken are: the
long pilgrimage over velvety moss and dry footpath to the
Abernethy Forest, out to the marshy ground leading down
to the Ryvoan Pass, and thence along the Lairig an Laoigh
as far as Derry Lodge. It is difficult to strike the proper path
through the wilderness of small lakes, and easy to go too
far up the hillside where one is obliged to traverse a desolate
plateau covered with desperate heather which clings and
impedes the way, before one comes to the broad track leading

27 SUMMER IN THE CAIRNGORMS : The Ryvoan Pass

THE LAIRIG GHRU PASS AND THE POOLS OF DEE, IN THE CAIRNGORMS

past the end of Bynack More. The path is at no point difficult, however, even where it joins the Avon and climbs up through the narrow cut between the symmetrical mountains of Beinn Mheadhoin and Beinn a' Chaorruinn and descends abruptly to the scattered trees lining the Derry Burn and finally to the ancient forest opening on Derry Lodge. This path must be followed not so much because it approaches Braemar through the heart of the Cairngorms, as because it leads to two of the most exciting walks in Britain.

The first one, which was traversed in some extraordinary fashion by Montrose, with an army, offers no concessions whatever to the most determined adventurer. It is a bitter struggle from beginning to end. It goes along the Water of Caiplich and the Ailnack Gorges to Tomintoul. The second, more sedate and more familiar, closely follows the Avon under the shadow of Beinn a' Bhuird, past the forbidding precipice of the Slochd Mor and barnacled Ben Avon to Inchrory and thence to Donside.

Both those walks will be described later.

The other two expeditions which must be undertaken are: the Lairig Ghru from Aviemore to Braemar and the circular route over Beinn a' Bhuird and Ben Avon.

The least favourable time for enduring the test of the Lairig Ghru is when the sky is clear overhead, when there is no wind and the rocks in the centre of the pass, despite their height, throw back the heat and blind one to the impressive mountain formations. Then the distant peaks of Deeside are in a haze, intensifying the feeling of oppression and sheer physical exhaustion.

Equally disconcerting must be the passage in the depth of winter when the crags stand out from the snow and the eyes are strained and agonised by the glaring white and the shimmer of the distance. The walk should be undertaken on an early autumn day when nothing is certain and weather and landscape change at every hour.

One such perfect day survives in my recollection as a mixture of opposites, culminating in a fine sensation of achievement. The clouds were lying heavy and black over the whole massif and there was a menacing drip from the larches and pines on either side of the road which leads to Coylumbridge, when I set out in the morning. The clouds broke to let blue, sharp-edged pools appear, enough to give encouragement without inspiring hope, as I went through Rothiemurchus scarcely receptive to the beauty of the ancient pines and not inclined even to look back on Speyside. As the road rose it became more and more marshy, even though it ran at a level above the stream and cut across the undulating plateau. To the left, the Lurcher's Crag shot up into the cloud, impressive in the uncertainty of rain and cloud and dwarfing the iron-grey bastions of Sron na Lairig.

As it entered the pass the road turned to the right, here one could look back on Rothiemurchus and Speyside, now a narrow strip of watery blue touched with a line of gold, where the sun, breaking through a barrier of clouds, shone on the remote mountain ridge. It was dark in the pass as the clouds came down and the peaks disappeared. The rain, which began uncertainly in heavy drops, changed into a vicious downpour and became a blizzard at the mouth of the glen where, beyond the Pools of Dee, one leaves the wilderness of boulders and begins to trace out vaguely a marshy path on the slopes left of the river Dee. Up from Mar Forest the blizzard tore, scouring every rock and every hill-face in Glen Dee. It howled round the summit of the Devil's Point and darkened the high, scooped-out corrie on Cairntoul. This part of the journey round the edges of Carn a' Mhaim was tiring and dreary, the road having degenerated into the bed of a persistent little river which filled the holes behind heather clumps and softened smooth sections of peat into quagmires, sometimes almost a foot deep.

When at last I got past the Devil's Point and looked towards the flat tops of Monadh Mor, closing up the forbidding end of Glen Geusachan, redeemed only in part by the harmonious grouping of Beinn Bhrotain, and had my first glimpse of Deeside to the south, the sun had pushed through the darkest clouds and fell on the distant landscape in a glorious shimmer of blue, unbelievably strange after the gloom and bitterness of the pass behind. The road continued round the face of Carn a' Mhaim, full in the sunshine, which did little, however, to dry up the marshiness of the road. When I got down to Glen Luibeg and the flat green meadows beside the stream, broken only by a solitary tree, the heat was overpowering and the feeling of oppression and fatigue increased. When Derry Lodge was reached, with a prospect of six more miles over a hard road to Braemar, I felt inclined to regret the snow and the rain and the cold of the pass.

Instead of taking the path down to the Linn of Dee, I held straight on, dodged round the edge of Mar Lodge and reached Victoria Bridge, where I hoped to slip through without difficulty. But full in the middle of the bridge stood a gentleman in a tweed suit of a perfection of fit, who read me a lecture on the rights of private property and the danger of trespass and was all for sending me back to the Linn of Dee, but at last he relented and let me get on to the main road. This was my first experience of a country which, in the vicinity of Braemar at least, is haunted by the guardians of private property, who classify ramblers with rabbits and owls as unnecessary vermin.

One had the impression of a special dispensation ruling over the destinies of the fortunate inhabitants of Deeside, an impression intensified as one gets closer to Braemar and becomes less intimidating as one leaves Braemar and moves along to Balmoral Forest.

At one time Braemar and the district must have been exceedingly beautiful, with magnificent larches and pines and occasional oaks and beeches, but the process of deforestation, which must now be almost complete, has left ugly scars and gaping wounds of rock on what must have been at one time graceful hillsides sloping to the Dee, which even time will have some difficulty in healing entirely.

Most exciting of any of the adventures in the Cairngorms is perhaps that which begins at the opening of the Slugain Glen, just across the Dee from Braemar Castle, and ends at Ben Avon. The southern end of the glen is no different from any other glen opening out into plantations, but it is made attractive on a hot day by the road which leads at intervals through dark, cool aisles of tall pines, intervals which heighten one's appreciation of the bands of glaring sun between.

The top of the glen is a paradise of grass, so fine and pure in colour that one hesitates to walk over it, and of birches, which throw complicated patterns of shadow. A group of deserted buildings stand at the head of the pass which, on wild nights, would be a refuge if one were courageous enough to force open a window or push through a door. The mountain slopes on either side come closer and closer to the road, forcing it eventually into the appearance of a defile with no outlet. This impression only lasts for a short time, and one emerges into an open landscape ending in a semicircle of great peaks to the north. To the west the eye glides over the steep valley of the Quoich which, broken by plateaux, disappears in the perspective of scanty forest and featureless mounds of hills.

One can follow the path to the right or cross the Quoich Water straight ahead, and go up a white stony path which becomes at times a deep trench cut through heather until it mounts the west shoulder of Carn Fiaclach, and enjoy the view of the mountains which guard the approaches to Deeside. The road from this first plateau to Beinn a' Bhuird is distinct and not difficult, and in the last stages it passes across terraces of loose rock in an advanced state of disintegration and leads out to a rocky plateau weathered almost flat and not unpleasant to walk on. The south top of the mountain lies at some distance from the middle of the plateau, and a few yards beyond it one has a view of the main Cairngorm ridge, as extensive as and perhaps more intimate than that from the lower slopes of Carn Dearg Mor beyond Aviemore.

The mountain slopes in the immediate vicinity terminate in a wide, flat stretch of moorland, a monotonous and uniform foreground to what appears in the hazy distance an unsubstantial background of folded mountains. Here one can see the cliffs on the east face of Ben Macdhui, the corrie high up on Cairntoul, and no more than a bare suggestion of a wall rising beyond Loch Avon.

Leaving the south top, one can either go to the edge of the cliffs surrounding Coire na Ciche or cut straight across the plateau to A' Chioch, where cliffs a thousand feet high move in a majestic semicircle round a deep loch, while a wider semicircle of cliffs edges the north top of the mountain. There is no more majestic sight in the whole of the Highlands than this terrific mass of cliff ranged symmetrically in constant threat to the two little lochs facing defiantly the solid bulk of Carn Eas beyond the valley of the Quoich. This experience is enough for one mountain, and the climber should be content now to go round the last semicircle to the little peak of Cnap a' Chleirich and thence down the steep slopes of the glen to the path at the bottom.

At isolated places round the edges of the corries the rock is reared up in gigantic masses of horizontal block, which, as on the farther side of Loch Avon, are so regular as to appear a deliberate act of construction; they push their faces right down into the bottom of the corrie and are unclimbable even by the most expert and most courageous mountaineer.

But the finest experience is reserved for the end. If, instead of going down to the path, one continues to a narrow neck at the very head of the glen, one comes out on a desolate corrie, the Slochd Mor. Its loneliness is such that even the

29 THE CAIRNGORM RANGE, from across Strathspey, showing the Cleft of the Lairig Ghru Pass

30 THE VALLEY OF THE FINDHORN, LOOKING TO THE MONADLIATH HILLS

mind can scarcely absorb it. There are no paths through this
wilderness of weather-beaten rock which sweeps down in
great curves and shallow glens to a hesitant stream. In summer
there is no water here and no relief to the fierce wilderness
of stone, the dazzling grey of the rocks throwing a frieze of
sharp edges into the sun-filled air.

Along the top of this wilderness one can traverse the
various tops of Ben Avon or climb the easier blocks of
granite which sit like warts on the face of the plateau, the
largest being more than a hundred feet high.

From Ben Avon, one could try a difficult descent to Loch
Builg, but it is not worth the effort. Better to return to the
narrow ridge called the "Sneck," go through the glen to
the path at the bottom, pass the great procession of corries
and come to the greenness of Glen Slugain, and in its quiet
coolness remember exquisite detail of light and colour which
had been lost in the confused sensation of overwhelming
majesty and splendour.

CHAPTER III

CLUANIE, GLENSHIEL AND THE
NORTH-WEST HIGHLANDS

HE was sitting in a deep arm-chair, partly in shadow, with the firelight outlining a bulbous nose and a grey beard tufted and uncertain in silhouette. What he had to say to us was far removed from the quiet room which sheltered us from a storm of wind and rain. He was recounting in immense detail the habits of the Eskimos in North Greenland. He had the art of story-telling and in the howling of the wind it was easy to believe the Eskimos to be with us. The function of this old Glasgow business man in our lonely Highland inn was to be our library and encyclopædia, even though a little judicious questioning brought out the fact that he was a constant reader of the *American Geographical Magazine*.

Another member of the company belonged to the teaching profession; he came year after year with his son to fish the waters of the Cluanie Loch, a pursuit with a reward as elusive as the blue bird of the Romantics or the Holy Grail. He was overjoyed that night because the storm, came after a period of drought which had dried up the rivers and clarified the lakes, and he foresaw bumper baskets in the morning and, his dignity relaxing in the warmth of the fire, he even made his contribution to family life among the Eskimos.

The day brought occasional visitors. Two old ladies, who arrived by the post-bus with the intention of going down the glen to cross to Skye and thence to Harris. The ordinary individual might have some difficulty in finding a way to the Outer Hebrides on a vague service of post-buses, but not the two old ladies. The usual string of young couples making a tour of Skye on their feet, shod for easy wandering over the South Downs. One afternoon, in a blizzard of peculiar violence, two handsome youngsters made their appearance, wishing to be fortified by tea before going straight over the mountains to Glenelg, guided by an inadequate half-inch map.

31 THE DRUIM PASS, ON THE BEAULY RIVER, EAST ROSS

32   A LARCH WOOD, KINLOCHEWE, WESTER ROSS

The hostess did all the cooking and she could cook a meal as no meal has ever been cooked before, perhaps because the inn was supported by a small farm which supplied it and made it independent of outside and more savoury and luscious things. That inn was a magic place: one would come of an afternoon along a lonely road across a deserted landscape, with nothing visible anywhere but an eagle rising out of the corries of Aonach air Chrith, expecting to enjoy tea alone and find a crowd of travellers who had presumably risen clean out of the earth—but then there was good reason for their appearance! The hostess baked all the bread and cakes and scones, and every day her supply would disappear long before the "tea" came to an end, the last-comers having to be content with plain bread. I have never known anyone who had a finer touch for sandwiches; it was almost worth going away for the day, if only to the moor behind the inn, just to enjoy them.

We all disappeared in the morning by eight o'clock: the business man to some obscure haunt down the glen; the fisherman with his ghillies, encumbered by paraphernalia of modern sport at a high valuation, down to Loch Cluanie; and myself to the peaks of Glenshiel and the Cluanie Mountains.

That inn at Cluanie remains in my recollection as one of the blessed places on earth. It was little more than a whitewashed cottage, two storeys high, with the roof encroaching on the top storey; it had a wooden extension where one could lie at night and hear the pattering of the rain above and of rats below.

This inn is typical of what one can find in the Highlands, in the remote districts west of Inverness and Ross-shire, and along Speyside and Donside. It has nothing in common with the tin-consuming boarding-houses of the more sophisticated centres or with the splendid caravanserai of the Trossachs and the easy uplands of Perthshire. It is associated with what one most willingly remembers of the old spirit of the Highlands not yet extinguished by defeat or by base commercialism.

Cluanie is one of the most remote and romantic corners of the Highlands, even though it stands midway on the road from the Great Glen to Skye, and the Cluanie hills are not inferior to the Cuillins or the more fashionable peaks.

The journey from Speyside to Glen Moriston is one of the most strenuous and probably one of the loneliest in the

F

whole of the Highlands. One can attempt the first part of it by going along the good, solidly built road from Newtonmore to Laggan, following the trace of what must have been the road built by Wade after the first Jacobite Rebellion; from Laggan onwards the road continues, still passable and still well-built, south of the river and along to the ford at Melgarve. After that, it becomes a difficult and speculative adventure across the Corryarick Pass, down the last steep descent to Loch Eanagan and Fort Augustus. The wise man would in any case provide for transport as far as Laggan Bridge, because the landscape, despite the frowning slopes of Creag Dhubh, beyond Newtonmore, and the precipices visible through the wood beneath Cluny's Cave, is one of the least exciting stretches of the river Spey. From Laggan Bridge the road continues on the flat, with a few switchbacks, through fairly rich farm country, past the forest-covered slopes of the mountains surrounding Loch Laggan, past Glen Shirra, with its loch withdrawn from the view of the wayfarer, and edged by carefully tended pine-woods, and comes to its first spectacular moment at Garva Bridge.

There the mountains come down in sheer precipices almost to the river side; to the south they are a broken wall of crag and cliff, with the corries of the high Laggan Hills springing out abruptly into sky. To the north one looks into a desolate glen and beyond a pine-covered knoll, to a waste of mountains, featureless and forbidding, which comes to an end on the slopes of Glen Markie.

Beyond the ford at Melgarve one can either take the Wade road, which is easy for the rambler and superficially attractive as it runs straight into the hills, or go to the left by a marshy footpath along water meadows to an isolated bothy at Shesgnan. Here the Spey performs such a complicated series of convolutions and is fed by so many streamlets that it is difficult to keep close to it, but the struggle is worth the effort, because in a short time one comes in sight of Loch Spey and at the same time discovers solid footing along what was once a cart-track leading to a deserted farmhouse. The cart-track goes easily up the hillside above the loch, offering a continuous view of all the streams that run in white tracks down from the Laggan Mountains to feed the Spey, and of the sharp block of hills rising in a solid wall straight to the south.

Beyond Loch Spey the track becomes a clearly defined route, and goes over a steading where the landscape reminds

33   SPRING IN BADENOCH : Loch Ericht, looking to Ben Alder, Perthshire

34 LOOKING UP THE GREAT HIGHLAND RIFT : Loch Ness, from Knockie Forest, Inverness-shire

one of the pure harmonies of colour described by Morris in his poetical novels. On the left rise the first lines of the "raised beaches" of Glen Roy, just a faint shadow hovering across the mountain slope, and as the hills come crowding on the river, forcing it into a narrow defile with rocks overhanging the road and topped by forbidding crags, the raised beaches come closer and the eye can follow them away into the far distance.

Down at Leckroy, with its quiet pastures beyond the encircling river, which has cut a way for itself under a tussocky plateau, one enters the heart of what might have been at one time a great lake, which has left, in subsiding, parallel beaches behind it. At Leckroy one can take a track leading straight down Glenroy, its parallel roads becoming more and more clearly visible until they intersect at Glen Gloy and reach the shores of Loch Lochy. Or one can be more adventurous and take a less certain and interrupted path over to the river Turret, where the parallel roads disappear, thence over a wet and difficult moorland to the waters of the river Sithein, down to an opening cut through the forest, and thence to the main road at Laggan Locks. From the last slope one has a first magnificent view to the south-west of Loch Lochy, with a very distant suggestion of Ben Nevis and to the northeast of Loch Oich, cut off by a series of lower peaks which come close to the lake.

Straight in front, over a tumultuous plateau, one can see the mountains of Loch Garry, and on clear days perhaps a suggestion of the highest of the Cluanie Hills.

From Fort Augustus one can travel by a car or by bus up to Invermoriston, and go thence through a densely wooded area as far as Torgyle Bridge, where the forest comes to an end—or take the old military road, built probably by one of Wade's lieutenants, to a flat upland about 1300 feet high. The road continues over a deeply embedded river and along a stony monotony on the other side, to a hillside broken by little clumps of trees where the deer take refuge. Straight ahead rise the broad slopes of Glen Moriston, culminating in the blue and vaguely majestic Cluanie Hills.

From Achlain to Ceannacroc Bridge the road runs through a green country, a river moving quietly to the right and the hillside rising flatly up, as devoid of features as an old lichen-covered wall. At Ceannacroc Bridge one can brave a notice, as one enters a cool birch wood, and go up the glen to the right and on to the marshy and boggy remains of the old military road leading to Cluanie, and then to Glenshiel. It must have been very difficult to make this section of the road, as the ground is full of bottomless bogholes covered with green grassy scum. At Loch Cluanie the landscape becomes wild, with the high mountains of Ceannacroc Forest rising in a steep wall to the right, peak succeeding peak, until they swerve round to a semicircle on the right and disappear in the direction of Glen Affric.

To the left, beyond the loch, rise the smooth slopes culminating in the clearly defined twin peaks of Bunloinn Forest, a well-protected and severely preserved shooting area. About three miles beyond the difficult entrance to the lake one passes the Tomdoun road, and thankfully reaches the inn.

On the whole, the journey from Fort Augustus into Strath Cluanie, despite the distant views of the Great Glen and the mountain tapestry hung across the end of Glen Moriston by the Cluanie Hills, is only moderately exciting, mainly due to the fact that there is no alternative of a good footpath to a hard and difficult road; but the latter only serves to heighten by contrast the wonder of the Cluanie Hills. One has only to go along the Tomdoun road for about a mile and look straight down into the valley stretching beneath a collection of peathags and bogholes and across an unstable sea of colour surrounding the pines of Cluanie Lodge to the deep defile leading to the upper waters of the river Affric; see the smooth green slopes of Am Bathach springing above a sparse forest like the prow of a ship cutting through the waves, with the sharp peaks of Ciste Dhubh cleaving the clouds behind it, and the great mountains to the right of the defile rising in immense waves broken at the crests, to feel the power and the glory of a great occasion.

This landscape is different from that of the Cairngorms. The latter had magnificent harmonies of delicate grey and purple and fine yellow and brown. The hills here riot in strong green colours, vivid dark purples, blacks and intense browns and live in a fury of strong light. On those grassy walls, smoothed out miraculously by a master craftsman and rising to sharp ridges with no corries or precipices, there should be multitudes of sheep and cattle living on a wealth of green herbage, but they are held desolate as if they were barren, icy stretches in the centre of Greenland.

From the inn one can begin to climb at once and waste no effort in traversing dreary stretches of hard road or lengths of heather-obstructed footpaths. One can begin the climb by going up Glen Caorunn Mor, which bends to the left about a mile on the road towards the loch and is one of the principal footpaths in the region. It has all the characteristics of a Highland track. It wanders at times all over the hillside, gets lost, becomes visible again where the bottom of the valley is broken by small plateaux of gravel and after three miles comes close under the shoulder of Ciste Dhubh. At that point one could make straight for the hillside, which is here slippery grass, perfectly dry, pull oneself strenuously over a series of shoulders—a characteristic of all Cluanie hills—and reach the sharp, well-balanced peak of Ciste Dhubh.

From that point one has the most comprehensive view of the mountains bordering Ceannacroc Forest: to the east the Five Sisters of Kintail and to the west Sgurr nan Ceathreahmnan and the giants of Glen Affric, Mam Sodhail, Ben Eige and Tom a' Choinnich.

The Five Sisters of Kintail rise in silhouette against the sun, a serrated wall of shadow with a gleaming river moving past them into the distance. Benn Attow, a shapeless lump of hill when seen from the upper waters of Glen Affric presents, across a deep valley, a shapely headland terminating in a sharp peak rising at the edge of a steep semicircle of smooth, grassy slopes.

To the east the mountains present an even more magnificent aspect; the group rising to A' Chralaig is a bastion of dark blue and grey, too steep to give a secure hold even to the tough grass of the Cluanie district, and the narrow ridge of the Mullach Fraoch-Choire, which throws against the sky a long series of sharply defined rocks. Beyond the upper tributaries of the river Affric rises one of the great mountains of Scotland, supporting with a mighty shoulder at its western end a beautiful, symmetrical peak. Few people climb Sgurr nan Ceathreahmnan, but it gives one of the finest mountain panoramas in Scotland, and looks down on the whole of Glen Affric, past Mam Sodhail over the two lochs, deep into the heart of the birch and pine forest which obscures the wide opening of the glen.

After this initiation into climbing, one can attempt something more spectacular by going along the Cluanie road, about a mile beyond the glen, leading up to Ciste Dhubh and cutting across the hillside to the left; for the first few hundred yards one must toil through sticky heather, alternating with patches

of stiff, reedy grass, but shortly one comes to a well-defined
deer-stalker's path, which goes in easy turns up the face of
the hill, and near the top moves straight across the contour
to the pass Coir a' Chait, the centre of loneliness and desolation, where mountain slopes swing up to the pass and high
plateaux, dark and marshy, disappear in the stern projections
of the Sgurr nan Conbhairean. From the top of this forbidding peak one can go north along a narrow, precipitous
ridge as far as Tigh Mor na Seilge and east to Carn Ghluasaid,
a reasonably strenuous walk, which seldom goes below the
3000 contour. From the top of the pass one reaches the first
stony slopes of A' Chralaig, the highest of the Cluanie Hills.
From the height of A' Chralaig, which is not by any means a
difficult mountain to climb, one can, on a clear day, get a
wide-spreading view of the lower hills bordering Glen Affric
on the south, and of the green, open meadows of the glen
and its two lakes glimmering in the distance.

The descent from A' Chralaig down to Glen Caorunn Mor
is more difficult than the ascent, if one is to avoid going
back *via* the Coir a' Chait pass. The grassy slopes are cut by
paths of sharp, loose rock, and the grass itself rises in deep
tufts which may conceal small watercourses with exasperating
efficiency.

The strenuous traveller, determined to bring to a test all
his physical resources, can go along the entire ridge to the
south of the Cluanie Forest from Creag a' Mhaim along to
the Bealach Duibh Leac, a distance not short of eight to
nine miles. A path leads across the Bealach from Glenshiel
to Loch Quoich and Glen Garry, but this ridge is so magnificent that it should be enjoyed in sections. It yields little to a
sated vision and a tired body.

One should go up the Tomdoun road for about four
miles, and, after due deliberation, for this country is heavily
protected by gamekeepers, get on to the deer-stalker's path
on the far side of Creag a' Mhaim and go in easy curves
right up the steep hillside to the top. From the cairn one
has a remarkable view, not only of Glen Moriston in the far
distance, but also of the narrow and deeply indented Loch
Loyne beneath, and the tree-enclosed water of distant Loch
Garry.

One can descend fairly rapidly from the cairn to the
narrow ridge of a mountain unnamed on the map, and have
a magnificent view to the south over sheer walls of rock a
thousand feet high, overshadowing a jet-black lake; from

35   IN ONE OF SCOTLAND'S LOVELIEST GLENS : Loch Affric and Mam Sodhail, Inverness-shire

36 LOOKING ACROSS LOCH DUICH TO THE FIVE SISTERS
OF KINTAIL, WESTER ROSS

37 GLEN SHIEL, LOOKING TO THE SADDLE, WESTER ROSS

this peak, which is little more than a knife-edge, one goes to the right, down the inviting slopes of Druim Shionnach, anticipating an easy descent to the inn, but Druim Shionnach makes no concessions whatever. It is built up in a series of almost perpendicular terraces where one must climb down narrow cliffs, which cannot be avoided, until one comes to the footpath beyond the marshy confines of the loch and descends thankfully, completely tired out, to the main Tom-doun road.

The central part of the ridge is approached most easily from the Glenshiel road, just where the old military road meets it and the battle of 1719 was fought. There is a description of that battle in Marshall Keith's memoirs:

THE BATTLE OF GLENSHIEL.

"The tenth of June [1] the enemy appear'd at the foot of the mountain, and after having reconnoitred the ground he attacked a detachment we had posted on our right on the other side of the rivulet commanded by Lord George Murray, who not being succour'd as he ought, was obliged to retire but without any loss. At the same time our center was attacked and forced with very little loss on either side; and after a skirmish of about three hours . . . our troops were forced to retire to the top of the mountain, whose height hinder'd the enemies pursuit. By this time it was night, which gave the chiefs of our party time to consult what was to be done in this urgency, and on considering that they had neither provisions nor ammunition, that the few troops they had had behaved in a manner not to give great encouragement to try a second action, it was resolved, that the Spaniards shou'd surrender, and the Highlanders disperse. Don Nicolas Bolano, who commanded the detachement of the regiment of Gallicia, offer'd to attack the enemy once more; but the general officers judging the attempt in vain, the first resolution was followed, and accordingly next morning the Spaniards surrender'd on condition their baggage shou'd not be plundered, and every body else took the road he liked best."

There is no road on to the ridge to the south, so that one must follow the river-bed up a series of terraces which become steeper and steeper until, in a last terrific urge, they break over a narrow ridge and sweep down in a stony precipice to the upper waters of the Quoich Burn. From this narrow ridge, which mounts sharply at intervals of about

[1] 1719.

half a mile to well-defined peaks, the highest of which is Sgurr an Lochain, one moves in a glory of mountain landscape so rich and so confused that one cannot retain any definite image of anything. At the point where one reaches the ridge, a deep glen opens beneath with the well-balanced mass of Sgurr a' Mhaoraich overtopping every other hill to the left, overshadowing even the Buidhe Bheinn which guards the approaches to Loch Hourn on the right. From peak to peak the path goes along the ridge, interrupted occasionally by small rock tors, and the mountains to the south come so close that the glen between is forgotten and the eye strains over wave after wave of rock until the clouds melt shadows, lines and masses into a delicate shimmer of infinite space.

At the highest point of the hills at the eastern end of the ridge, Aonach air Chrith, one looks across to the deeply indented buttresses of Gleouraich, rising into sharp ridges with a solitary cairn balanced perilously at one end. Beyond it, to the right, lies the mysterious water of Loch Quoich, and to the left the lower slopes of Glen Quoich Forest fade away from Spidean Mialach past a terrific wall of rock down to the richer surroundings of Loch Loyne and the upper waters of Loch Garry.

To the north the whole magnificent range stretches in an unbroken series of smooth waves rising at times to sharp crests from the Five Sisters of Kintail, where they overshadow Loch Duich, to the high mountains forming the Ceannacroc Forest beyond Loch Cluanie.

In front the main buttress of Aonach air Chrith rises abruptly to a castle of rock, and then rushes down almost to the inn; standing on that castle, one can see all the great buttresses and bastions which support the range on the east and on the west until they disappear in the wilds of Glenshiel. Beneath, the slopes go past great masses of isolated rock into a rocky amphitheatre, where there is only the thin sound of water dripping from a height and a subdued flapping of wings.

The extreme western end of the ridge is blocked by the Saddle, a worthy rival of the Five Sisters of Kintail, stretching in an iron wall on the far side of Glenshiel. From the bridge one gets a first glimpse of the Saddle, a serrated mountain which concedes nothing in magnificence or difficulty to the more fashionable peaks of Skye.

The only path which gives any hope of access to the Saddle

38 LOCH QUOICH, SOUTH-WEST INVERNESS-SHIRE

39 THE HEAD OF LOCH DUICH AND THE KINTAIL HILLS, WESTER ROSS

goes off to the left, deep in Glenshiel, beyond the Mhalagain River. One can see the path quite clearly from the road as it goes diagonally straight across the near hillside, away from the smooth, almost perpendicular slopes of Faochag, a dark grey and purple fortress growing sheer out of the main mass of ridge. The path emerges on a plateau which yields, to the south, to the first vague boulder-strewn approaches to the Saddle. One can make straight for the centre of the ridge or compromise by going up the less obvious route along a narrow stream and thence, after a succession of insecure terraces fixed on rock, to a narrow platform which leads ultimately to the summit.

In that way one misses the difficulty and danger of the sharp crest which gives on the centre of the ridge itself, and is the obvious means of approach. Any satisfaction one can have at escaping this difficulty disappears in the task of getting up to the summit, because there is not a yard of its route which requires anything but a good sense of balance and sure footing. The rock rises in masses of masonry which are interrupted frequently, forcing one down sharp, narrow descents and up more forbidding walls still, and on to places where the influence of rain and wind has been such as to force the rock masses asunder, throw them down on either side in ruin and leave the traveller a knife-edge of ridge with a precipice on either side as his only path.

The summit is comparatively flat and easy, but beyond it one engages again in a long series of struggles with sharp rocks, yielding to repellent and nerve-testing ridges, until the climb comes to an end at Spidean Dhomhuill Bhric, and one can enjoy at ease what is perhaps the greatest reward that the Cluanie Mountains can give.

Straight below, with practically no divergence from the perpendicular, the corrie drops like a gash in the mountain-side, a thousand feet down, to a little green loch; beyond it the eye travels over the lesser slopes of mountains converging on the calm waters of Loch Duich. To the west the sky is filled with Ben Sgriol, balancing a little white cloud on its majestic, symmetrical top. Beyond Ben Sgriol one sees a line of silver, which is the Sound of Sleat, and beyond it a tenuous, shadowy line, without any definition—the mountains of Skye. The light of the sea brings the whole of that mountain mass into silhouette so brilliant that the edges stand out as sharp and as definite as if they had been printed on the sky in black.

G

To the south one can see a circle of light just visible between the masses of rock, the lonely waters of the loneliest and most unapproachable loch in Scotland—Loch Hourn. Beyond it, to the south-west, is a confusion of shadowy forms of the precipices of Luinne Bheinn, and beyond it again to the south, in a very faint patch of colour, the high mountains which close up the end of Loch Nevis and swell down in great folds to the waters of Loch Arkaig.

To the east the view of the Five Sisters of Kintail is shortened by the plateau dominating the west side of Glenshiel, and one has a sensation of unreality as those evenly serrated peaks rise in a uniform stretch of colour above the foreground, which has no definition beyond masses of rock thrown beyond the edge of the plateau.

One can traverse the Five Sisters of Kintail from the first unnamed peak above the Coirein nan Spainteach (named after the battle with the Spaniards which took place at the foot in Glenshiel), or go east from that point as far as Sgurr an Fhuarail, which juts out over Strath Cluanie and gives a long, thin view to the loch and the glen beyond.

Or one can go into Glen Affric and struggle up the un-exciting, if steep, slopes to Ben Attow. The great moment of the Cluanie Hills and the mountains around Glenshiel is along that great ridge to the south which has been described already.

There was a typical Robert Houston omnibus-picture, "By Morar to the Sea," full of light and blue colour and a somewhat spurious attraction of easy drawing and semi-dramatic light and shade, at the 1935 Exhibition of the Glasgow Institute. Compared with the usually gloomy and dark original it appeared frail and insubstantial, but in one respect at least it touched on the real beauty of those great Highland lochs opening on the sea. From Loch Linnhe northwards the lochs are irregular gashes in the mountains, secluded and unapproachable; but if one should stand on a mountain beside them and look west to the Atlantic, one would discover that in some magical fashion their harshness has disappeared and their engulfed inner light is so intense that everything else is subordinated to it, and every detail of the landscape assumes a new and strange life. The sandy beaches shine vividly in contrast and the distant hills across the sea are refined to a blue shadow, less substantial than the water from which they rise.

40   LOCH HOURN AND THE HILLS OF KNOYDART, INVERNESS-SHIRE

41   LOCH HOURN, LOOKING TO DRUIM FHADA, INVERNESS-SHIRE

One can go from loch to loch after many strenuous journeys and find that they have this surrender to atmosphere—an ennobling and yet a softening influence—and so one is tempted to suggest that the most effective way to approach those Highland sea-lochs is from the sea itself.

Loch Morar can hardly be considered a sea-loch at all, joined as it is to the sea by what must be the shortest river in Scotland, but it has all the characteristics of a sea-loch. It is separated from the Atlantic by flat stretches of beach, and its mountains are conditioned, to one observer at least, by the reflection that just behind them stretch the immense blue waters of the Atlantic.

From the shores of Morar one looks out to Rhum and can enjoy, night after night, magnificent sunsets. There is nothing finer in the whole of Scotland than this succession of coloured scenes suspended across the sky. The lake itself, one of the deepest on the West Coast, is as tightly bound by lofty mountains at the eastern end as Loch Hourn farther north. It is overshadowed here by the crescent of mountains, acting also as a barrier to the upper waters of Loch Arkaig; the mountain slopes come down into the water with no poise in their movement, the upper folds tumbling over to form what looks from the distance gloomy precipices, and the highest point of all to the north is Sgurr na Ciche, just visible beyond the abrupt near shoulders, a sharp-pointed mountain which gives character to the less overwhelming and more serene landscape visible at the end of Loch Nevis. On the south-eastern end of the loch the two peaks, Sgurr nan Coireachan and Sgurr Thuilm, form a high plateau on which the heavy rain-clouds beat when the storms sweep up from the south.

Loch Nevis, separated at Tarbet by only a narrow neck of land from the last loch, is a more peaceful stretch of water, its beauty being more finely displayed by the comparatively easy slopes of the near hills. The two even peaks of Luinne Bheinn and Meall Buidhe, less lofty than Sgurr na Ciche, bring a symmetrical conclusion to the landscape and give harmony to the almost artificially arranged lower slopes of the southern end of the loch.

Luinne Bheinn in turn dominates Barrisdale Bay and is one of the peaks visible in the distance from the top of the Saddle in Glenshiel. Luinne Bheinn is seen in its finest perspective from Lochan nam Breac, one of the loneliest lochs in the wilds of Knoydart; it forms with Ladhar Bheinn an immense wall silhouetted so steeply against the sky that

Loch Hourn is only a thin blade of light, lost in an immensity of shadow.

Loch Hourn itself is probably the most impressive of all the sea-lochs, as it is the most unapproachable. On the north the water runs close under the steep slopes of that fine mountain Ben Sgriol, swerves round the terrific slopes of Druim Fada, which is in turn dominated by the serrated peaks of the Saddle group and then disappears in a narrow mountain gorge blocked up by the bulk of Sgurr a' Mhaoraich.

This mountain series, right from the edge of the sea round to the mountains overshadowing Loch Quoich, must be one of the most impressive mountain areas in all Scotland, and one of the least accessible.

Loch Duich, which is the next northward loch beyond Loch Alsh, is less gloomy and threatening because the Saddle group shades off to long, rolling slopes on the south of the Five Sisters of Kintail, which are held in a perspective so open that they have more of a decorative Japanese quality than of Highland truculence, even though Glenshiel is a narrow defile as imposing as anything to be found in the vicinity of Loch Hourn.

Loch Alsh is even less impressive, but it has its own measure of beauty because of its background of the hills of Skye. The coast itself is so twisted, so full of little bays, with trees dotted pictorially among them, that the artist's enjoyment of it can only be rivalled by his pleasure in Loch Nevis or Loch Morar.

One can go beyond Loch Alsh north to Achnashellach Forest and follow a cart-track which leads alongside the Allt-a-Chonais east to Glenuaig Lodge, and emerge after many miles at Loch Beannacharain, thence along a rapidly widening glen to Strath Conon and finally into the smooth meadows surrounding the approaches to Strathpeffer and Dingwall.

Farther north still lie two of the finest mountain and water landscapes on this west coast, and both are dominated by the same group of mountains. Loch Maree, which has its finest representation in a picture by Horatio McCulloch, is a narrow, straight lane of water many miles long, accurately cut through the heart of the mountains; it is a sheet of silver reflecting back the terrific buttress of the Slioch, which rises from the water in a gloomy central mass, supported on both sides by beautiful pointed shoulders. On the south it reflects

42   LOCH MORAR, with its family of small Islands, Inverness-shire

43 LOCH EILT, with its many islets, Lochaber, Inverness-shire

44　LOCH MAREE, from the Seaward End, near Poolewe, Wester Ross

45   THE GATEWAY TO THE HEBRIDES: Loch Alsh, with Eilean Donan Castle in the foreground, Wester Ross

the high Beinn Eighe, which balances in the distance the mass of the Slioch, with a suggestion farther west of the sharp peak, edged with crags, of Beinn Alligin.

Beinn Eighe, with its precipices and its pointed towers, bears a point of resemblance to the Saddle, but it is so enormous as to be not far short in sheer bulk of Bheinn a' Bhuird. This group of three—Beinn Eighe, Liathach and Beinn Alligin—similar in form with their square blocks of masonry, their symmetrical peaks spaced off in horizontal terraces across the sky, the powerfully massed slopes which come rolling up to the high walls with little gradation beyond, have a gloomy magnificence which even the sun-swept waters of Loch Torridon do little to diminish. They shoulder aside the clouds and impose silence and gloom on a loch which, to the south, has the character of a delicate pastel.

From the entrance to Loch Torridon and the north-west corner of Loch Maree, their bulk is as an upheaval of nature, violent enough to make the rocks force themselves through the immense masses of granite. All of them can be climbed with comparative ease, but they impose their own conditions of weather and storm and their precipices will give the practised mountaineer all the effort and all the muscular strain he may desire. The less expert traveller, moving up the glen from Loch Torridon to Loch Maree, might feel vaguely intimidated in the shadow of those great peaks.

On the way to the fishing at Loch Maree, who cannot remember the dreadful pot-holes in the road as soon as one took the left hand of the fork road shortly after leaving Garve? It was improved in later years, when the County Council of Ross and Cromarty had saved up sufficient funds to construct "passing places," the length of the road to Achnasheen (pronounced locally and therefore properly, with a long A). Was there ever a Gaelic name, meaning "Field of Rain," more appropriate?

But for a long time the road from Achnasheen to Kinlochewe at the head of Loch Maree, by Loch a' Chroisg's side was full of "craters," like a road in Flanders in '14–18. These rough roads were not so severely felt in the days of the old "mail gig"—now succeeded and superceded by the motor coach—with a change of horses at Kinlochewe, some nine miles from Achnasheen, and again at Loch Maree Hotel, ten miles farther on, on the way to the Coast at Gairloch village, on Gair Loch, twenty-eight miles from Achnasheen.

The first, much-looked-forward-to sight of Loch Maree, after the steep, winding climb from Loch a' Chroisg to the head of Glen Docherty, must have many a time given the returning Scot a bitter disappointment, so often is the glen head steeped in "haar." But if the weather conditions are favourable, the sight of the islands jewelled in Loch Maree, with Isle Maree dividing the north-west end from the south-east, is a sight never to be forgotten. Passing down the loch the ten miles to Loch Maree Hotel, for there is nothing but the hotel there, one gets a first glimpse of the perfect setting in beauty of the many islands.

Kinlochewe, at the head of the loch, renowned for its brilliant flower gardens, is a famous fishing centre. In former years each boat had two ghillies. These were essential owing to the distance from the hotel of the fishing water, some beats being some four miles down the loch, and others more than that up the loch, and to the gale which springs up with little or no warning, not even to the ghillies.

Now the introduction of outboard motors makes one ghillie sufficient. But where the successors to this grand body of men are to come from, is a question which is causing the fishermen folk great concern. The "Number 2" in former years was the "makee learn," but now no young men are taking to the boats. The season is a short one, from mid-July to the "back-end" of September for salmon and sea-trout, including that delectable little one-year-old called the "finnick."

Some years ago now there was an intense competition to get to the favourite spots first to try to ensure good "baskets," and the hotel staff were being asked to get up earlier and earlier to provide breakfasts, so that ultimately they had no time left for sleep between finishing off the previous night's dinner and getting ready for the next meal. Consequently, some of the "old timers" got together, possibly because their years were getting on, and they themselves found the time in bed all too short, and arranged for a surveyor to "lay out" the loch in "beats." There are some thirteen of these. The beats are not numbered in any consecutive order; No. 11, "Coree" is, for instance, at the northernmost end of the hotel water, while No. 7, "Salmon Reach," at the other extreme, is separated by about seven miles on a compass course. In this way the "changes are rung," according to weather and other conditions, thus avoiding "sameness."

46 AN ARM OF THE SEA : Loch Nevis, on the west coast of Inverness-shire

47 SHIELDAIG VILLAGE AND LOCH TORRIDON, WESTER ROSS

48　WINTER SNOW ON BEN SLIOCH, with a glimpse of Loch
Maree, Wester Ross

49　COIRE NA POITE, a Corrie among the Applecross Hills, Wester Ross

On arrival a fishing guest takes whatever beat is vacant on the roster. Each day he deducts—not adds, as in the '14–18 years—one to his number, when he becomes No. 1, he goes to the foot of the roster as No. 13 and works his way back, so that a fortnight's fishing covers all the water.

The beats vary from loch-side stretches to island clusters. There is much of beauty for the fisherman, and for others, on non-fishing or "blank" days. Isle Maree is the burial ground of a Danish Prince and Princess, whose gravestone is marked with the Celtic Cross; here, too, is the "lucky" tree, in whose dead trunk every one who lands upon the island hammers in a copper penny, no other coin will suffice to bring, or at all events to "guarantee" good luck. There is an oasis of white heather on Isle Ruairidh, or "Big Rory," while Isle Gubhaim has the "Lily-Pond" islet, full with water lilies, and a smaller loch within it, which in turn has an islet all of its own contained inside it. On beat No. 10 there is "Armoury Point," called "Fools' Rock"—just why, most fishermen wonder! This point is said to have housed claymores and targes, put there when Prince Charlie passed through these parts.

A mile or two farther down the Loch from the hotel is the stone where Queen Victoria loved to go down of an evening and watch the sun setting at the foot of the Loch, behind Loch Ewe and Lewis.

For non-fishermen, and even for fishermen on a "blank" day, there is the hill loch, Loch Garbhaig, about three-quarters of an hour's walk up the hill, at the back of the hotel. On a clear day the sea at Poolewe, at the head of Loch Ewe, and the Minch are easily visible: it makes a never-to-be-forgotten spectacle, surrounded, as one is, on all sides by still higher mountain ranges stretching away to the Torridon Hills.

If the day is "blank," and the fisherman is far removed from the hotel waiting for wind, the time is delightfully spent yarning to the ghillies. Nearly all of them were in the R.F.R. or R.N.R.(T.) during the War years, and most of them live round Gairloch or Loch Ewe. Ian Dhu ("Black John") has his home on Isle Ewe in the middle of loch Ewe, and, it is said, never leaves his croft from one fishing season to another. He claims descent from the Spaniards who were wrecked there after being storm-tossed after the Armada. "John" is another old crony: still a bachelor, "Not," as he says when the query about marriage is put to him, "but what I'm not fit."

A mile or two down the loch there is a cluster of delicious wild raspberries on the side of the Slattadale Stream, which flows out of Loch Garbhaig, a short way up which are the famous "Victoria Falls." On the north side of the Loch is the famous deer forest round Slioch Mountain.

The road from Loch Maree Hotel to Gairloch leaves the loch-side near Slattadale and winds over the hills down by Kerrysdale, passing on the left the fork road which leads to Badachro, a tiny clachan at the south-east corner of Gairloch, which well rewards a run down to see it, to be enchanted by the dulse colouring on the rocks around the tiny harbour; then farther on past Flowerdale House, the home of the Lairds, the Mackenzies, and on and up alongside the beautiful sandy bay into the village of Gairloch.

The two remaining lochs which must be visited on the west coast are Loch Broom and Loch Assynt. Both Little Loch Broom and Loch Broom are dominated by the great peak of An Teallach, a mountain which repeats on a much greater scale the steep slopes and serrated tops of the range between North Goatfell and Cioch na h-Oighe, in the Isle of Arran. There are no smooth corries here, but abrupt and sharply cut slopes with deep couloirs and inaccessible slabs, verging on precipices. The mountain is seen at its best from Loch na Shellag, but even beyond the plateau which descends abruptly to the upper waters of Little Loch Broom, it presents a terraced wall so clean cut against the sky as to appear several times higher. One might almost think one was in the Bernese Oberland surrounding Kandersteg.

The most difficult peak of An Teallach, Sgurr Fiona, gives from its last serration one of the finest panoramic views in the whole of this area. One can look across to the marshy, mountainous plateau beyond Ullapool, and pick out against the sky the amazing series of behemoths which ends at Quinag across Loch Assynt. The high shoulders of Beinn Dearg rise so steeply that they seem a continuation of the mountain. Beinn Dearg, one of the highest mountains in the North of Scotland, rises in an enormous dome, with buttresses coming down in steep terraces to Glen Broom itself; it is seen at its wildest and most impressive from the foot of the Loch a' Choire Ghranda, since its steepest corries come down here in a straight line to the water. Beinn Dearg looks south across

50   THE JAGGED RIDGES OF THE TEALLACH HILLS, WESTER ROSS

51 LOCH BROOM, from above Ullapool, looking to Braemore Forest, Wester Ross

desolate rolling uplands, with occasional high shoulders projecting from them to the solid, shapeless mass of Ben Wyvis, which, even at that distance, has only bulk and little symmetry.

The last loch, namely, Loch Assynt, is not a sea-loch. Standing on its shore near Lochinver one can see rising above the dark, flat moorland an astonishing succession of isolated mountains, islands of rock rising like prehistoric monsters under parallel straths of cloud. They are spaced out at almost equal distances, beginning with the more conventional humped mass of Quinag, and passing thence south of Loch Assynt to Canisp, with its long tableland, terminating in a smooth peak, and an abrupt descent at the south side. Closer to the view, and "end-on," rises the sharp hump of Suilven, narrowing to a crest at the top; beyond Suilven, Cul Mor, Cul Beag and Stac Polly. Of all these, Suilven is the most remarkable, but Stac Polly with its sheer precipices facing the long, flat plateau of Ben More Coigach, is a perfect conclusion to the rock-bound, torn-up and storm-stressed coast.

Suilven is one of the most difficult hills to climb in Scotland, owing to the sharp approaches to the main peak and the narrow, serrated ridges which rise like " aiguilles " in a rhythmic succession from west to east. Quinag, seen from Canisp, rises blackly above Loch Assynt in a landscape which has no sign of life or vegetation in it. It is rough hewn out of the beginning of time.

Stac Polly, silhouetted against Ben More Coigach, has a violent upward suggestion which is emphasised as one goes slowly up its steep sides beyond the carefully graded rock and scree slopes and emerges on the crest with an immense view of Loch Lurgain, the islands round the entrance to Loch Broom and the tormented coast which reaches far beyond Lochinver. It shares with Suilven this vision of loch and river, patterned on moorlands edged by the distant cloud-strewn sea.

Beyond Loch Assynt itself, deeper inland, stands Ben More Assynt, a high hill with sloping corries grouped in a crescent round the inevitable small lake. It is more conventionally shaped than the strange monsters farther/west, but with the group of lower hills to the north, it gives character and force to what would otherwise have been a dull and featureless lake, Loch Shin.

The two remaining peaks in Sutherlandshire, Ben Hope

H

at the south end of Loch Hope, and Ben Loyal which stands
sentinel to the Kyle of Tongue, are set in an immense, desolate
moorland country which gives to them, through the force of
perspective, a deeper significance and a more splendid suggestion than they would have had in a more crowded landscape; they give an impression of greater force than the wall
of hills which lies at the foot of Loch Eriboll and continues
with occasional projections over a long plateau to Cape
Wrath.

The country near the head of Loch Erriboll is almost
wholly deserted and seldom approached, but it is a fitting
conclusion to a country of great mountain panorama and
great symphonies of cloud, sea and rock.

Farther south one can discover a great wealth of peaks
along the great glens which run from east to west: Glen
Cannich, with a long rampart seldom rising to magnificence,
which stretches east from Riabhachan to reach a single high
point at Sgurr na Lapaich; Glen Fanich, with its loch darkened
by the crescent of four peaks with their summit in the centre
at Sgurr Mor; and glen Strath Carron, which reaches west
through Gleann Mor to the high peak of Beinn Dearg.
Other and less exciting glens, such as Glen Orrin, complete
the tale of the east to west watersheds which run right
across the North of Scotland, each different in character
and beauty and each extensive enough to constitute a world
in itself.

And farther west, as one approaches the Atlantic shores,
barrenness makes way for fertility. To this country of Morar
and western lake-linked peninsulas one should come to steal
a march on spring, while snow still clothes every mountain,
and lochans and waterfalls in Cluanie and on the high peaks
are ice-bound and the day's lengthening has not reached the
gloom of the narrow ravines. Down to this warm sea-board
come the deer in mid-winter, "gate-crashing" if necessary
into gardens, but generally finding abundant nurture in the
beautiful mosses, green, pink and red, which fill the woods.
Here growth never stops, primroses come in December and
the birches hang out their tassels when the country inland is
still winter-gripped.

It is an abundant and fertile land: in autumn the rowans
droop heavily from their branches and the hedgerows are a
tangle of luscious brambles, hips and haws, fuchsias, late
honeysuckle, ferns and mosses of infinite variety.

Grass verges, smooth as velvet, edge the roads; trees grow

52 LOCH LONG, where it joins with Loch Alsh at Dornie Ferry, Wester Ross

53   BEN MORE COIGACH, from Loch Baddagyle, Wester Ross

54   CUL MOR AND AN STAC, from Inverpolly, Wester Ross

55   SUILVEN, most spectacular of Sutherlandshire peaks, from the East

56   THE LANDSCAPE OF SOUTH UIST: Loch Einort, looking to
Ben More

57   THE ROCKBOUND COAST OF GRUINARD BAY, WESTER ROSS

58 THE SUTHERLAND LANDSCAPE : A lochan, near Rhiconich

59   THE WILDS OF SUTHERLAND : Ben Loyal and Loch Hacoin

60   THE KYLE OF TONGUE ON THE NORTH COAST OF SUTHERLAND

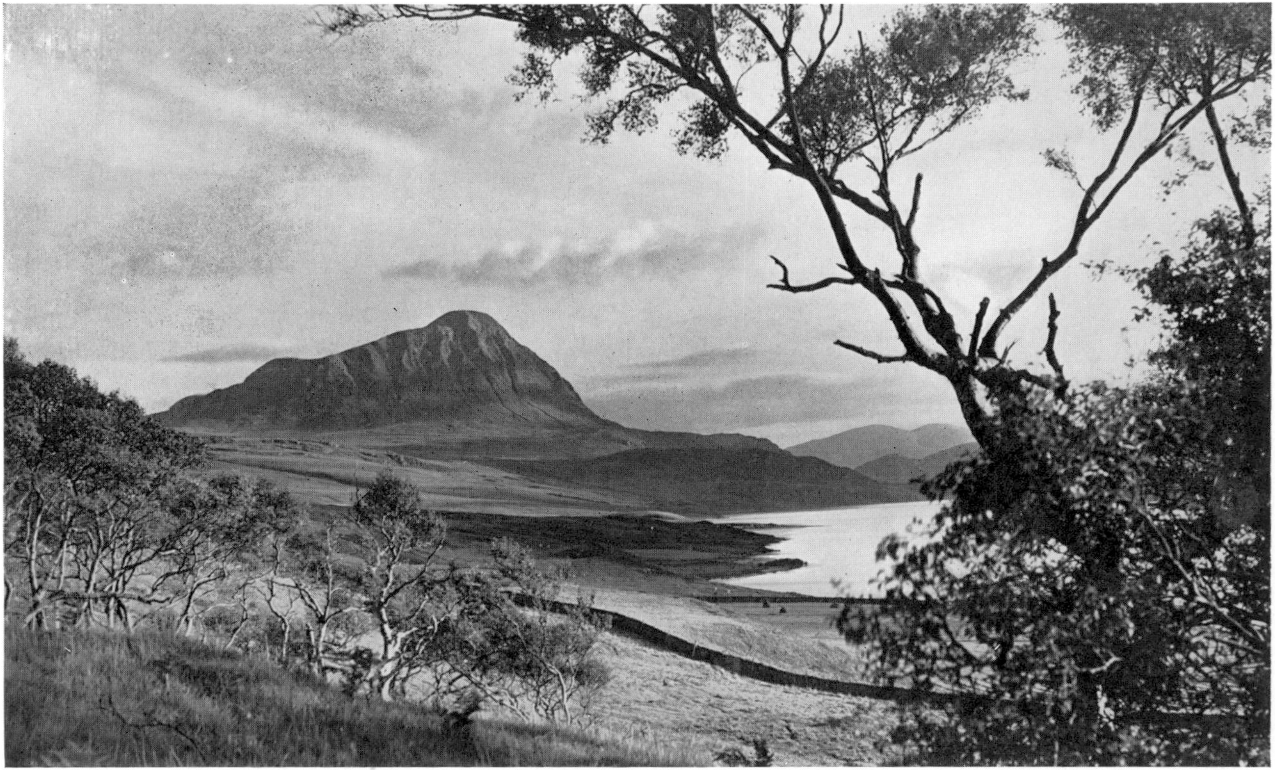

61 BEN HOPE AND LOCH HOPE, NORTH SUTHERLAND

down to the shore and at Morar's outlet bend over the sea-water as it flows swiftly and quietly over the silver sands to meet the onrush of the short, glass-green river which, crashing over its falls, brings the overflowing waters of the inland loch to the sea.

CHAPTER IV

ARRAN, SKYE AND THE ISLANDS

My first recollection of Kilbrannan Sound and of Kintyre is a very faint one—just a picture of a boy standing behind the easel of one of the veterans of the Glasgow School, painting on the beach at Carradale, sharing instinctively the view of the old fishermen who wondered whether it would not be better if the picture were like the place.

Carradale was always an enchanted spot because it was always so full of picturesque figures, not so much the conventional bearded artists as the weather-beaten fishermen and the Gaelic-speaking individualists who clustered round the pier, went out at night in their boats to secure uncertain catches of herring, tanned their nets in great boilers on the rocks and hung them on lofty frames to dry in the wind and the sun.

I remember listening, fascinated, to the groups of blue-jerseyed experts holding lengthy conversations in Gaelic, which were quite unintelligible to me, but occasionally they condescended to exchange some rude anecdotes in Celtic English, and they always made a point of practising to the full, when the pleasure steamer called at the pier, the peculiar type of Highland humour which consists in making outrageously disparaging remarks about the personalities of the most decorative uniformed commanders.

The more practised among the individualists did not trouble to go out in a fishing boat—they preferred to do a little careful netting and poaching for salmon and river trout on the Carradale River, despite the threats of an autocratic old army officer, who exercised an intensely feudal supervision over the whole district.

Kintyre and Arran, in those days, were primitive places. They shared, for example, the services of one doctor, who would be rowed in an open boat across the sound from Carradale to Blackwaterfoot in Arran. In Campbeltown by

62   ARRAN FROM THE MAINLAND

63 AN ARRAN CROFT NEAR HIGH CORRIE

the Sound of Kintyre, miles beyond the picturesque and ancient Saddell Castle, life was fuller, but on the whole more sordid, because it was, even in the earliest days, a poverty-stricken settlement, living on a combination of two decaying industries: distilling and sea-fishing. Occasionally the warships would anchor in Campbeltown Loch and play their searchlights by night over the surrounding districts. I have still a recollection of a romantic expedition when we went fishing for salmon and sea-trout, whiting and lythe, and got mixed up in a school of porpoises and actually saw a whale in the far distance, outlined against the sunset. There was one infallible bait for sea-fishing: an artificial fly made with the white hair of the wild goats which are still to be found on the higher and more deserted peaks of the peninsula.

Davaar Island, with its painted crucifixion, had its own power of suggestion, and the fishing boats could always group themselves into a picturesque composition, which became utter confusion when a Russian tramp steamer came into the port and lay there waiting for an adequate load of salt herring. The entire town at that time seemed to be submerged beneath a sea of barrels, and one stood in a mushy, slimy mess of small herring, thrown out by the women salting and gutting on the pier.

One could climb the uplands to the north of the town and gain a splendid view of the ships passing up the sound, with the hills of Arran silhouetted like a blue drop-screen behind. Or go right across the peninsula to Machrihanish and, running along its endless stretches of smooth sand, watch great Atlantic rollers coming in, with all the verve and magnificence which so attracted painters of the quality of MacTaggart and Henderson.

Occasionally one attempted a more ambitious expedition to Southend, one of the historical corners of Scotland, where, at the Rock of Dunaverty, a peculiarly horrible massacre of Covenanting times took place. This massacre is described by a contemporary writer:

"We beseegd Dunavertie, which keepd out well enough, till we stormd a trench which they had at the foot of the hill, wherby they commanded tuo stripes of water. This we did take in the assault. Fortie of them were put to the suord. . . . After this, inexorable thirst made them desire a parley. I was ordered to speake with them; neither could the Lieutenant Generall be movd to grant any other conditions, then that

I

they sould yeeld on discretion or mercy. . . . At length they
did so; and after they were comd out of the Castle, they were
put to the suord, everie mothers sonne, except one young
man, Mackoull, whose life I begd, to be sent to France with
a hundreth countrey fellows whom we had smoaked out of
a cave, as they doe foxes. . . . Mr Johne Nave (who was
appointed by the commission of the kirke to wait on him
as his chaplaine) never ceased to tempt him to that blood-
shed . . . and I verilie beleeve that this prevaild most with
David Lesley, who looked upon Nave as the representative
of the Kirk of Scotland. . . . Bot I reallie beleeve, advise
him to that act who will, he hath repented it many times
since, and even very soone after the doeing it."

One of the early Celtic saints landed at this point from
Ireland and one of his footprints is still shown in the
stone.

On a clear day, one can stand on the rocky coast and see
the coast of Ireland rising beyond the Atlantic, an outline
of low hills, and if the rollers are quiescent, one can get over
to Sanda Island, an attractive plateau, cropped by sheep and
haunted by myriads of seagulls.

Kintyre is full of little legendary and historical associations and events just sufficient to give a spice of adventure
to a landscape which, dominated by the presence of the sea,
yet contrives to be imposing and beautiful.

I have had as much pleasure wandering over the untrodden
hills behind Carradale, none of them of any great height, as
I have had in the more lofty peaks projecting above the island
opposite, and there are few beaches so fine as that of Carradale
Bay, with its strange shellfish and its glistening white sands.
The sun appears to rest on the eastern side of the peninsula,
even when it is obscured, and there is a wealth of almost
tropical foliage, especially in the vicinity of Campbeltown,
which must appear strange to a visitor from any other part
of the British Isles.

Beyond Kilbrannan Sound, one can go by road over to
the shores of Loch Tarbert and thence by easy stages past
Lochgilphead up the famous Loch Fyne as far as Inveraray.
The best way is to go by boat, since the landscape on either
side of the loch, pastoral, smooth and peaceful as it is, is
only a foreground to a colourful series of hills which form
an almost continuous background on either side right up to
Inveraray.

More picturesque, and more frequently visited, are the

64   THE COAST OF LORNE, WITH THE CLIFFS OF EASDALE, looking to Mull, Argyllshire

65   THE PEAKS OF ARRAN : A view from Goatfell

66   GLEN SANNOX, ARRAN, looking to Cir Mhor

lochs which open out on the Clyde estuary; Loch Long, which stretches up to Arrochar, with the mountains rising abruptly to the much painted craggy towers of the Cobbler, the three peaks of Beinn Ime, Ben Vane and Ben Vorlich interposing a high rampart broken by two steep glens.

From Arrochar, one could pass over to Loch Lomond and go along the lakeside by a singularly unattractive black tarred road. The views from the slopes above Ardlui down the whole length of the loch, with Ben Lomond rising smoothly into the sky to the east and the white water broken by green islands fading off into a light-dimmed flat distance, have a quality rather finer than the more spectacular and confused panorama visible from the top of the road which leads, after many windings, from Arrochar round to Inveraray. Loch Lomond is only partially in the Highlands, although its upper reaches can be as gloomy and as magnificent as any other loch in Scotland.

From the south one approaches it through the industrial slums of Alexandria and the sordid pier of Balloch: unattractive in the extreme. Once in the loch, however, one can go easily and happily up to Inversnaid and thence along a simple, well-trodden path to the top of Ben Lomond, and look over the whole of the Clyde estuary, over to the Campsies and south to the peaks of Arran, down to Aberfoyle and across the lowlands as far as the Ochils on a clear day.

The Campsies themselves have a special quality because they give a feeling of clean, beautiful distance beyond a filthy, black, industrial landscape. The only comfort I had when, during some part of my life I was condemned to live at Coatbridge, with its stinking dumps of slag, was to stand on the hills just outside the town and look across the distance to those fine mountains; in the early spring especially, when the sun rested on the snow and the shadows were incredibly blue.

If one has courage enough to penetrate as far as Strathblane and the Clachan of Campsie across the intervening industrial landscape, with its coal mines, one can wander over this singularly beautiful country, with the hills just high enough to let one into pure air and give one a magnificence of views over the Lowlands of Scotland.

Kilbrannan Sound and the Clyde Estuary have their finest ornament in the Island of Arran, a source of inspiration for the last hundred years for the Scottish schools of painting, innumerable poets, writers and geologists. The peaks of Arran, like the peaks of Skye, are not among the highest in Scotland, but next to those of Skye they are the most impressive. Goatfell, the highest point, may only be 2866 feet, but every single foot, from sea-level upwards, tells in the final effect.

(i)

Arran, until very recently, was an interesting feudal survival. Owned by one great family, a great part of its communal life came under a form of control which might have been current about a century ago, but no longer corresponds to the times. Sunday, for example, is still a day of rigid adherence to Church ceremonial, with a paralysis of all activities which have even a remote connection with enjoyment. The entire island, with the exception of one centre, has been completely teetotal: a matter of little consequence for a population which is still capable of ingenious and advanced methods of smuggling.

For this very reason Arran is fascinating. It has an independence of character combined with a romantic defiance of the law. The austerely dressed villagers and fishermen, walking along the coast road to the lonely church, may gaze down with easy toleration on the squalor and disarray of a gypsy encampment. The local baker may instinctively recognise the necessity of some kind of obedience to the traditional house, but has no objection to debating at the top of his voice in your hearing whether he should give a mere tourist morning rolls or not.

As a result of this comparative immunity from the influence of fashion and a somewhat sordid commercialism, the island still possesses many beautiful villages. Brodick may have all the appurtenances of sophisticated leisure, but even Brodick cannot escape the influence of the majestic mountains behind it, and one has only to go along the coast to a little place like Corrie to enjoy the old simple living. Lamlash and Whiting Bay are rather less interesting because they have not the merit of magnificent landscape to act as a background to their commercialism, but the former looks over to the Holy Island and has at times the excitement of a visit from the Fleet. The whole of the south and west coasts is completely unspoilt, and even Blackwaterfoot, defaced by a flurry of badly-designed bungalows, has preserved so much of its old individuality as to be able to give some merit even to those additions.

The most delectable part of the island lies undoubtedly between Lochranza and Dougrie, with its finest point at Catacol, the two Thundergays and Pirnmill. From any of those points, as from Corrie and Sannox, one can penetrate easily to the higher parts of the Island which lie north of the String, the road which cuts across from Brodick to Blackwaterfoot. A more conventional jumping-off place is Corrie, mainly because it is close to the Goatfell group, but much the finest, from the point of view of natural beauty and strength of suggestion, is Catacol.

Catacol, with its quiet row of twelve houses, lies at the foot of a steep glen which runs right back into the mountains of Arran, and it is down this glen that those sudden squalls come which are a danger to shipping on the Kilbrannan Sound. At night, during the summer and autumn, when the day temperature is falling, short-lived storms of terrific violence invariably occur, but they serve to keep the air exhilarating and are in themselves an inspiration.

Up Glen Catacol one follows a broken stream, and after about three miles emerges on a plateau. Most of it, unlike other parts of mountainous Arran, is rather pleasant walking. From this plateau, which is a watershed for two rivers running north and south and has no paths running through it, one can shirk any further effort and go north to Loch na Davie, which lies in a close defile between the outliers of Caisteal Abhail (peak of the Castles) and Beinn Bhreac, the finest peak of the flattish range which comes up in a steep wall towards Glen Catacol and forms a solid mass behind Loch Ranza. From Loch na Davie one goes over wet, tufted ground along by a river until the hills close in, and at the top of a steep wooded slope one can look down on the old castle of Loch Ranza and across the Kilbrannan Sound to the sun lying on Skipness. This corner is entirely satisfying from the pictorial point of view, as it has a suggestion of strength, although everything is on a small scale.

From this plateau one can go down Glen Iorsa, which is practically a continuous bog and one of the most disagreeable and difficult walks in the whole of Britain. The plateau, however, is a means of access to the one attraction of the landscape: straight in front to the east, running north to south, stretches a mountain wall which is not far short of the Cuillins in the abruptness of its precipices and the severity of its features.

One can follow this range from the first narrow slope at Creag Dhubh to the high point of the Caisteal Abhail, then down to the pass at the top of Glen Sannox, up again to the majestic pyramid of Cir Mhor and farther down to the confused mass of A' Chir, which is like an immense wall with whole sections missing out of it. Beyond lie the smooth slopes of Beinn Tarsuinn, and south of Beinn Tarsuinn comes a narrow peak above a long crest, Beinn Nuis. Beyond this peak, the wall rises to a lesser headland and comes down again into the plateau.

One can traverse the whole of this ridge, which covers about six miles, without serious difficulty, A' Chir providing some very pretty rock-climbing. Or one can branch off at Cir Mhor and pass to North Goatfell and thence down to Brodick.

The wise man who prefers a succession of magnificent pictures and experiences to one indigestible confusion is well advised to take those mountains one at a time, because at no moment do they repeat themselves and there is not a single monotonous stretch.

On one day I climbed up the smooth, steep slopes of Caisteal Abhail, a company of deer appearing for a moment on the skyline, and reached the first splendid point where the masonry blocks form the peak of the Castles. The view from this point is probably the best in the whole of Arran. To the east, out to Kilbrannan Sound, the landscape stretches in a series of well-defined humps, and beyond Loch Tanna rises a group of mountains like an island above a larger plateau. Beyond those mountains, again, rise the slopes of the Kintyre Peninsula, and beyond that, in a faint light, the Paps of Jura—a decorative contrast to the terrific precipices, steep slopes and sharp peaks of the adjacent mountains. Down the side of the peak of the Castles, past a sheer cliff hundreds of feet high, one looks to the head of a wild glen which forms, near the sea, a quietly exquisite pastoral scene.

Glen Sannox is enclosed by a narrow crescent of high peaks which sweep round in steep walls to end in high craggy bluffs to the north at Suidhe Fhearghas, and on the south at the sheer wall of Cioch na h-Oighe. To

67 THE PAPS OF JURA

68 THE ARRAN HILLS ABOVE GLEN ROSA

69 " THE ROOF OF MULL " : A view from Ben More

the south, almost within touch, rises the granite monolith of Cir Mhor, Goatfell appearing dimly beyond its shoulder.

The peak of the Castles discloses what is even finer— an immense panorama of sea and land bathed in a blue and golden shimmer where Ben Lomond is a small blue shadow on a silken haze and the Cumbraes are just green enough to be distinguished from the blue of the sea. One can look right into the heart of Loch Fyne and see islands, lochs and peninsulas spread out in a pattern which is the storied beauty of the Islands.

From the summit of the Castles, one may attempt a descent into a curious cleft, Ceum na Caillich, which gives the mountain its characteristic appearance from a distance, and thence along the ridge to Suidhe Fhearghas and across to Glen Sannox, for it can be climbed from almost any point, however forbidding its appearance.

On the west side A' Chir is guarded by wet, smooth, dangerous slabs which are almost unnegotiable; occasionally they make way at the top for broken ground with tufts of grass in between. If one is unwilling to face the precipitous clefts in the mountain wall, one can go straight down on the west side. The most difficult moment occurs near the Bealach an Fhir-Bhoga, where the fall on the east side assumes the appearance of a vicious precipice. Beyond that point one can climb on to the top of Beinn Tarsuinn or, after some steep rock-climbing, get on to the centre of the ridge and climb down over Beinn a' Chliabhain, past a series of granite projections to the highest point at the narrow southern end of the ridge and thence over a low marshy headland, Cnoc Breac, to the Garbh Allt, and thence down a steep glen to Glen Rosa.

The view from Beinn a' Chliabhain, past the terrific wall of A' Chir to the pyramid of Cir Mhor and round the top of Glen Rosa to the steep broken slope of Goatfell, is impressive and intimidating at the same time. There is no spot of colour to relieve the desolation of grey, broken only by the tumbling white of the water and the deep shadows thrown by the peaks across the corries. The defensive wall of Goatfell continues uninterrupted beyond the flattish plateau of Glenshant Hill and sweeps round the end of the bluff with no softening in its gradation.

Glen Rosa is wilder certainly than Glen Sannox, mainly because the green lowlands at the entrance to it are hidden, the mountains jutting out above with no relief of colour except the shadow of the rocks.

The third expedition was to the Goatfell massif. One can take the usual hackneyed road up from Brodick, clearly marked by orange skins and litter of all kinds, but one can do much better by struggling up Glen Sannox almost to the face of Cir Mhor, and then scrabbling up the hill to the narrow pass on the south-east. From that point one can ascend by steep steps to North Goatfell, which has a fine accumulation of boulders to form the high peak, and then go south to Goatfell, clearly visible beyond the involved path which comes down now on one side, now on the other, to avoid a series of "gendarmes."

Goatfell itself as a viewpoint is rather inferior to North Goatfell, mainly because it gives on a series of ridges with a single deep, penetrating perspective into Glen Rosa and across to the dark precipices of Coire Daingean. It does, however, bring into view the two peaks, Beinn Tarsuinn and Beinn Nuis, with Beinn a' Chliabhain spread out in front of them. To the east the whole of the Lowlands of Scotland and the Southern Highlands lie open to view as far as the eye can reach.

From the summit of Goatfell one should return to North Goatfell and strike across to the north-east, at right angles to the ridge which leads to Cir Mhor, to an unnamed high point a little less than a mile off. That walk is one of the finest things in Arran; it never ceases to be exciting, and is bordered by immense boulders of granite weathered into the strangest shapes which rear to sheer precipices. As one looks down on to the brown greyness, broken only by the river Sannox, the ridge dives down, narrowing almost to the width of the path before it reaches a broken, tumbled mass of rock at Cioch na h-Oighe. Beyond this bluff one descends by a number of hidden steps to Glen Sannox, or straight across to the woods bordering the main road near Corrie.

The farthest part of the Goatfell—Cir Mhor group—is the combination of Beinn Tarsuinn and Beinn Nuis. To diversify the approach I went to Dougrie on a somewhat doubtful day, believing that it would be possible to go up the Iorsa Water to Loch Nuis, but the experience proved unsatisfactory, mainly because the rain came down in a solid wall of misery after I had, with some difficulty, got about a mile up the glen. The moor was an alternation of burnt heather and green meadow, and the closer I came to Loch Nuis, the more difficult and the more impossible became the going.

Loch Nuis, a dreary stretch of water, with no shelter from driving rains, had little of interest in it; there was a fierce, cold wind blowing up the slopes, sufficient after a time when the rain had stopped to dry one's clothes and freeze one's nerves. From the top of Beinn Nuis, an easy climb, one looks down a drop of several hundred feet at the nose of Beinn Nuis, with the black clouds hanging over the Firth of Clyde and the rain squalling across the dreary picture of Lamlash and the Holy Island. To the east of Iorsa Water, the undistinguished top of Sail Chalmadale and the more symmetrical masses of Beinn Bharrain and Beinn Bhreac were a shifting blur of grey.

On a clear day the ridge walk from the cliffs at Beinn Nuis across to Beinn Tarsuinn would be stimulating, but in the semi-obscurity of a rainstorm it had a terrifying suggestion of immense depths opening on either side, and the descent to the Bealach an Fhir-bhogha was by no means simple. In the final stage one must clamber or slither down a singularly wet and disagreeable granite slab, with all the possibilities of a glide over the precipice. Beyond the pass one goes easily across a narrow neck of the shoulders of Beinn a' Chliabhain, with the shadow of the mountain slopes beyond the Coire a' Bhradain rising solidly against a loaded sky.

The only other mountainous part of Arran worthy of close exploration is south of Catacol and west of Loch Tanna. From Catacol one can go along the shore in the direction of Pirnmill for about a mile, and then traverse the bare moorland to the east of the shoulder which lies south of the highest bump of Meall nan Damh. From that point one can climb round the edge of a corrie with a loch at the foot. At one time, many thousands of years ago, this loch may have been surrounded by steep precipices, but they have been weathered to scree slopes broken by occasional boulders, with a single sharp edge along the top.

From the crest of that corrie one goes up steady grass slopes to the top of Beinn Bhreac, with Loch Tanna lying drearily below, then along an easy road to the top of Beinn Bharrain, with a sharp buttress jutting out from it like a wall pointing towards South Thundergay. At the end of the mountain group one can watch, under an immense over-

K

hanging table of granite, the ships passing down Kilbrannan Sound and clouds sweeping over the moors beyond Black-waterfoot.

The descent from Beinn Bharrain is not altogether pleasant, because at the foot of the buttress one must go over a boggy country, broken by shallow glens, for what appears to be miles before the smooth meadows of South Thundergay are reached.

One can go round the whole island by the coast road which goes through some beautiful country, particularly at the south end. In the vicinity of Kilmory, right along to Dippen, one goes through a countryside which might almost be in North Devon, and the coast itself breaks off into cliffs. But the splendour of Arran lies in the great massif which is crowned by the three peaks of Goatfell, Cir Mhor and the peak of the Castles. The last is perhaps the finest of all and it is well named "the sleeping warrior," because one can actually trace the form of this warrior as one goes round the headland before turning into the shallow bay at Loch Ranza.

(ii)

Of the other islands scattered in thousands along the West Coast of Scotland, the Outer Hebrides, particularly Lewis and Harris, Skye, Mull and Jura come most properly within the category of highlands. Islay, for example, and Colinsay, as well as Tiree and Coll, are on the whole low-lying, comparatively flat rock-surrounded masses, often with fine sandy shores and green pastures, but they have no outstanding features which would bring them literally within the category of highlands.

Islay is the largest of a small group of islands overshadowed by the neighbouring Paps of Jura, which rise to heights not far short of those in Arran. The highest Pap, at 2571 feet, is only a hundred feet lower than Goatfell. Islay is an extraordinarily pleasant place in which to spend an easy summer holiday, but the landscape is almost wholly pastoral, with occasionally forest, and so one must be content with gentle excursions over what is almost rolling downs and a magnificent sea beating all round.

Jura is not a very accessible island. It has only one small section of road round the south end; it has been kept rigidly preserved in the past and is even now, as far as one-half of

70 ARDMEANACH HEAD, on the western coast of Mull

71   RHUM AND THE SCUIR OF EIGG, from Morar Bay, Inverness-shire

the island is concerned, railed off pretty efficiently for deer-stalking purposes. The three high hills are seldom climbed, but they are famous in the history of Scottish painting, as they form the subject of one of MacTaggart's masterpieces and the background to seascapes so often put on canvas by MacTaggart's contemporaries and followers.

There are other small islands which share with Jura this power of bringing the world to a single point of vision. Gigha comes readily to the mind as a lonely deserted jewel of the sea. "Out of the world and into Gigha," a familiar saying in the west, tells more about it than any description. Rhum and Eigg silhouetted against the sunset, beyond the rocky shore of Arisaig or the white sands of Morar, are eternally significant. Rhum, not an easily accessible island, is dominated by the same type of deer-stalking exclusion as Jura; its four hills, Askival, Ainshval, Hallival and Sgurr nan Gillean, form a series of pillars which are difficult to climb but the view from the top of Askival over the contorted, confused, but colourful West Coast from Ardnamurchan up to Skye, with the Cuillins close at hand, is very fine.

The island which one associates with peace and cool, clear colour is Iona. One can visit it for the sake of its historical links, shutting one's eyes to the disastrous reconstruction of the cathedral. But one should revisit it as a serene, ideal resting-place, filled with the echoes of great seas borne on high-speeding winds in the full light of summer.

At the entrance to the Firth of Lorne there is a small group of islands, the Garvellochs, which have always attracted me because of their isolated position in the midst of intricate archipelago. Their little hills stand out defiantly against Ben More and its outliers on Mull. One can select innumerable examples all along the West Coast of this type of island.

The island of Mull has been made famous by the romantic explorers of Tobermory, in search of illusory Spanish galleons, and more recently by the paintings of Hughes Stanton which disclosed a more sophisticated type of beauty than one would expect in the Western Islands. Ben More, in Mull, is the highest point in the Scottish Islands, outside of Skye. It is easily approached from the birch-lined glen which runs south of Loch Bà. From its narrow peak one looks over an immensely complicated pattern of indented country, stretching beyond the northern circle of Mull and along the West Coast to Skye —if one can face up to the winds slamming round it. A less spectacular group of hills to the east, culminating in Dun-da-Ghaoithe, gives a view straight up Loch Linnhe into the Great Glen, with the Glencoe Mountains to the east and the distant masses of Mamore Forest blocking the skyline beyond.

The remaining islands are Lewis and Harris, with their extension south to the two Uists, Eriskay and Barra, and Skye.

(iii)

One has been so impressed by descriptions of the Cuillins and the more spectacular Skye landscape that one tends to forget their comparative insignificance in the make-up of the island, quite apart from the fact that the whole majestic group of the Cuillins would barely give feed to fifty sheep. They do not occupy in comparison to the total a very large part of the country, and they are all crammed together at the southern end.

Alexander Smith in his *Summer in Skye*, which is still the finest interpretation of Skye, attempted to strike a balance between the show places and the more stolid but, in its own way, just as picturesque background. Smith was not a mountaineer. He was a sociable person in the great tradition of Dr. Johnson, and it is only in a few places that he breaks out into magnificent description. He was enormously preoccupied with individual Skye-men, and he assembled a very full collection of local legends and anecdotes which have been the stock-in-trade of every Skye impresario ever since.

Now, owing to changes which have taken effect in the comparatively short period since Alexander Smith wrote, the old characteristics have tended to disappear and commercial exploitation of certain parts of the country has far advanced, but the great difficulty of Skye remains. One cannot recapture that world of easy social relationships and cordial human intercourse which has been associated with the purely literary side of Skye. A second Dr. Johnson would have some difficulty in discovering those rich characters and those solid social excellencies which were sufficient to obscure the misery of the rain and reduce the hardness and cruelty of the mountains to a dimly perceived, rather uninteresting geo-graphical background.

The modern generation is equally indifferent to manufac-tured solemnities of the Ossianic race. It does not question the authenticity of Macpherson's Ossian: it is simply not interested, and all the attempts to put a pretty decoration of early heroism and barbaric deities on the Cuillins and the hills of Skye are seen to be merely a veil over something much more splendid. It is not afraid of ancient deities and pagan superstitions; it tends to regard them as unnecessary relics; its sense of values has been so rudely shaken by the War that it measures by a very small gauge indeed the mighty exploits of legendary warriors. It is equally not over-whelmed by the bare majesty of the hills themselves—content to take them as they are, without frills or obscuring analogies.

This reflection does not, however, get us over a difficulty represented by Skye itself. The possibilities of recapturing the old literary tradition are practically gone, and one is not sure that even the historical associations and particularly the history of the Young Pretender's adventures have the force of attraction to the youthful mind they had some years ago. If one puts all this aside, one has still the physical difficulty of combining an easy, if temporarily arduous exploration of the high hills, with the much more prolonged and less spec-tacular enjoyment of a landscape which, at first sight, may be entirely repellent and uninteresting. Yet the time may come when the visitor to Skye may, like Alexander Smith, find greater and more lasting interest and attraction in the low-lands and the moor-topped and cloud-shadowed uplands, with the sea swirling round innumerable cliffs, sucking into innumerable caves and hollows and smoothing out innumer-able sandy beaches, than in mere rock climbing. To-day this betokens a more subtle appreciation of atmosphere and land-scape values. The Skye landscape is no different over a great part of its area from any green or pastoral landscape any-where else. It has its moments of utter desolation. It has its free ranges of space, but one can find in the Peak of Derby-shire, perhaps, an even more forbidding area than in the up-lands of Skye. There are certain qualities in it, however, which have an even more inspiring effect—at least in recollec-tion—than the vaunted peaks of the south.

One may find in Dunvegan and Loch Snizort, reflecting on a calm day the immense clouds over the Atlantic, and the uncompromising bulk of the Storr, a richness of beauty more finely to be appreciated than the bitter black or red mountains south of Loch Coruisk. The attraction of the western sea, edged in by the long, narrow line of the Outer Hebrides and brought to an exact limit almost at one's feet by the rocks and cliffs and beaches, is something that cannot be easily put away from the mind. It penetrates deep into that perception which is part of one's being and Skye, to a greater extent than any other island, has the power to revive and strengthen that influence.

A visitor may well content himself with an occasional stroll along the ridge which acts as a spine for Trotternish and find his great pleasure in wandering along the vitalising Atlantic seaboard. He will avoid places like Portree as being unworthy, but he will find a new pleasure in the lonely crofts verging on Loch Bracadale and Loch Eynort. He may still have some difficulty in waxing enthusiastic over the long mass of bumpy landscape which lies west of the Sound of Sleat and of the country surrounding Armadale Bay.

The reason for this is, of course, that the mountains round the great lochs running into the Sound of Sleat—Loch Nevis, Loch Hourn, Loch Alsh and its extension eastwards, Loch Duich, are so magnificent that the immediate Skye landscape appears as an anti-climax, and the Cuillins themselves are so dominating that it is only at Loch Eishort with their silhouettes in front that one can have any expectation of further beauty and of a new sensation.

This sensation will have little to do with the usual pictorial representations of the Skye mountains. There is a picture by D. Y. Cameron, which is almost entirely a harmony of greenish blues, exquisite in colour, beautifully brushed in, but there is nothing exquisite nor greenish-blue about the Cuillins. They are bitter, violent black or dark grey precipices; their harmonies are harmonies imposed from above, from the over-flooding sun or the over-shadowing clouds. They are conceived as terrible structures, all grey and black and torn red and occasionally green.

One steps out of the motor-boat at Kyleakin faintly incredulous that these round stones, green with water-weed from the lapping water, are Skye ground; or this white-washed, well-kept village a Skye hamlet of living beings—Presbyterians, perhaps, of the strictest Free Church, engaged in their human play, school-children who still must learn to count and keep

72 A HEBRIDEAN HERD AMONG THE ISLANDS

73   THE SOUND OF SLEAT AND THE CUILLINS, ISLE OF SKYE

account, and their parents who live by the island's name. Broadford, with gardens trimly set behind its dykes, straggles unpretentiously about its business; and Portree has at first sight a tidy, southern air, with its landlocked harbour and neat quay and terraced rows of houses a few steps from the water. At night, as you sit at the low window of a quay-side house, watching the faint thickening of the summer night where innumerable small craft lie moored, the water plucking at their sides in its rise and fall, the one ship's lights winking, a gull screaming suddenly and the dark outline of Ben Tianavaig rising across the harbour, the sense of small seaport intimacy known and loved from childhood counteracts any feeling of strangeness on this almost legendary island. But these homely ports do nothing to reveal the individuality and enchantment of Skye. Nor does the barren moorland which stretches in sombre folds over most of the interior of Skye, rising at times to shaggy heights, brown in autumn with the shades of old heather, bleached grass and withering bracken, relieved only where patches of ling or heather are still in bloom.

The seaboard road by Broadford to Sligachan, winding tortuously round sea-loch and glen, gives one giddy glimpses, here of a ruddy shoulder and over it of a black crest; then northwards, and the sun-shot loch is before you and Cuillins disappear; round again, and another wild ridge spins into view and threatening imminence.

As soon as one turns south from Portree in the morning or descends over the high moorland from the west, one sees the Cuillins on the horizon, irresistibly drawing the eyes. From whatever distance one sees them, the brittle-edged peaks rise, rough-sawn, from their long graceful flanks: nowhere could they be mistaken for another range. Perhaps the root of their individuality lies in the fact that from whatever angle they are seen they form a balanced and composite whole, all the peaks rising to about the same height, sufficiently close set to leave the pattern of the whole mass undisturbed—unlike the more ungainly, oddly dispersed mountains of the mainland, where one's vision is distracted by the neighbouring peaks. This compactness of the Cuillin group, standing clear above all else, lends them a sense of greater height and magnificence. First sight of them should always be from a distance: if mist shrouds them, wait for a day, if possible, before you approach.

High mountains the Cuillins are not, compared with the

thousands of feet that are reared up in Central Europe and Asia, but their precipices rise from deep glens or marshy flats, practically sea-level; the long-view shows them majestic in outline, in the near view they are overwhelming, even when their crests are hidden in mist. And yet, while climbing them, their precipitous compactness gives one an amusing feeling of being on a little playground. On a clear day, balanced on the ridge of Dearg or Sgumain or Alasdair, voices ring across with disconcerting clarity from figures as small as flies on the opposite faces of the hills and a descent on the Great Stone Shoot rustles through the neighbouring hills. The distances are not great from peak to peak, but they take some climbing.

An air view would give the impression of some Fingalian stag's antlers or the skeleton of a mammoth multipede, branching spurs joined at right angles to the main angles, with deep, ice-hollowed corries between. Beginning from Sgurr na h' Uamha, rising steeply above Harta Corrie on the north-east, the main ridge lies a little northward; it turns west on Sgurr nan Gillean with its four pinnacles, and still farther west to Bruach na Frithe; then south-east, falling into the main line of the hills, and down, through a succession of peaks, from Sgurr a' Mhadaidh to Alasdair, the highest, and Gars-Bheinn in the south. East of this main ridge, and parallel to it, forming the backbone of the great monster, is the straight line of Bidein Druim nan Ramh, the Peak of the Ridge of Oars, which sweeps threateningly, as from a high galley, down to the very water of Coruisk. Eastwards again from this is Blaven, one of the finest of the ridges, with its bow swell.

The Red Cuillins lie to the north of this general group of Black Cuillins, greatest among them being the reddish-yellow rounded humps of Glamaig and Beinn Dearg, whose granite composition has saved them from water and ice erosion. The mixed composition of the Black Cuillins, on the other hand, has

> "suffered a sea-change
> Into something rich and strange."

It requires little imagination to see the Cuillins in the ice-age, ice slipping down slowly from the peaks, leaving the crests vulnerable to the ravages of frost and whittling them down to skeleton form, while the corries were being hewn out by glaciers. These, with their cupped lochans and

74   THE PROFILE OF THE CUILLIN RANGE across Loch Eishort, Isle of Skye

75   SGURR ALASDAIR, the highest point of the Cuillins, Isle of Skye

76 LOCH CORUISK AND THE CUILLINS, Isle of Skye

precipitous drop, are typical of ice-weathered formation, and Coir' a' Ghrunnda and Coruisk especially, have the smoothly ground, rounded rocks indicative of glacier action.

"Black" the Cuillins are against the light or in stormy weather, but dark grey or purple generally; steel grey under a summer sky; bluish purple (quite different from the purple of heather) against the primrose sky of evening; and alternately red and black on their western face, the corries deep in shadow, under the brilliance of an Atlantic sunset; perhaps their colour is most delicate in late afternoon when the sky pales to almost no colour at all, and one is perched aloft in a maze of hills which graduate from silver through all the shades of purple and mauve to rosy pink, according to scree, boulder, rock or sheer precipice, and above all, the perspective of distance.

These hills are good for climbing. Those sound in wind and limb and properly shod, and those who do not lose their heads when momentarily no way up and no way down seems possible save for a lizard or an antelope, may climb most of the peaks in fair weather. Morning may be fine, with wisps of mist rising wraithlike from the corries, to disappear at last from the crests, but noon may bring showers of hail, rainclouds that drift with maddening stealth or, worse still, establish themselves in seeming immobility. For experts, virtuosi with rope and feet, there is excellent rock-climbing and strenuous ridge-walking—not on the backs of whales as in the Grampians and in the Inverness Highlands, but very often on a saw's edge.

The hills can be approached from the north at Sligachan, from the east at Elgol and from the west at Glen Brittle; and in most cases a strenuous walk is involved before reaching their base.

The easy northern peak of Bruach na Frithe, approached from Sligachan by A' Mhaim, lays northern Skye and the western islands and peaks at one's feet. When the sun has passed its height the rosy shoulders of the Red Cuillins stand bulkily out in front of the two sea-lochs, Sligachan and Ainort, the Narrows of Raasay and the wooded island beyond, and, over wider waters, one can see the hills of Applecross Forest, An Teallach and Liathach; westward are Lewis and Harris, a humpy chain; and, if one is lucky, St. Kilda. Immediately to the north lies the great headland of Trotternish with Staffin and the Quirang

L

visible and southward is a mass of broken ridge and corrie.

Any of the southern peaks—Alasdair, Sgumain, Dearg or Gars-Bheinn—raise one to a bird's-eye view of the islands: Gars-Bheinn preferably on a day of still clarity, when snail-like cumuli hang on the horizon and the indented coastal hills, flattened out to a shimmering line, are indivisibly joined to the arching sky and sea. Ben Nevis stands out, clearly the monarch. Gars-Bheinn, on such a day, towers above Loch Scavaig and Coruisk, quite changed from their customary menace into sheets of jade, where the white backwash of an excursion steamer is no more disturbing at this height than a snowflake. To the west hangs the pendant of the Outer Hebrides; and southward, wine-coloured Rhum and Canna and Muck; and close beneath, so that one might drop a pebble on it, green Soay. Skye is the axis from which the islands are flung out like sparks from a flying Catherine wheel.

This is what fine days bring, when the ridges are clear; but one may wake suddenly in the middle of the night and hear the hollow roar of the burns. Rain falling heavily after midnight fills them quickly to the lip, their colour changes from peaty amber to glass green, curdling to foam where the "force" crashes over an eighty-foot drop, cork-screwing savagely before it thunders into the deep pools. The ferns on either side flutter distractedly as the solid wall of water surges past.

On the western side of the Cuillin there are very beautiful waterfalls, particularly on the burn which comes from Coire a' Ghreadaidh and the Banachdich Burn. The former may mean "clear waters," and no name could be more aptly given. Pool after pool lies deep, cut in pale rock, so that the water appears in quiet weather like so many pieces of jade—blue, grey and green. In its lower course rowan trees and ferns grow on its banks. Here one must plunge into the cool water to understand the delights of a Highland burn.

One should see the fine sea-lochs which eat into the western coast, dividing the headlands, when the tide rolls in; or on an early morning, when the tide, having receded, hangs stilly in the balance, mirroring the opposing cliffs like a polished black tent. Towards the shore, copper-brown sea-weeds and dulse cover the low rocks, and gulls, at pasture, rise and scream echoingly in rage at some pilfering fellow.

77   PABBAY AND THE BARRA ISLES, OUTER HEBRIDES

78   A HEBRIDEAN WOMAN WITH HER PANNIERED PONY

79   USING THE CAS-CROM, OR FOOT-SPADE, in South Uist, Outer Hebrides

And on the shore Mackinnon, in plus fours, drives his five geese along the road; Mhairi leads in her calf to be fed; and the small lad with bare feet and grey jersey gives Gaelic salutation to his mother's neighbours in the little lochside village.

One can bathe in these lochs, "with nothing between you and America," where in sunny weather the water shows every rock, stone and plant in the bed below; or take boat round to the other lochs, Scavaig or Slapin, Eishort or Brittle, Eynort, Bracadale, Dunvegan or Talisker Bay, with some feeling of adventure on the long Atlantic swell. Or cross to the islands, Rhum and Canna, or to Soay, the nearest, where they pasture cattle behind the houseless, fern-lined harbour.

Or one can climb leisurely up the cliffs to the headland over Beinn an Eoin and down to the top of the seacliffs where the Atlantic beats; or to the moors towards Drynoch where there is no sound but the wind in the bent grass, curlews calling, and the sudden whirr of frightened wings startled out of their nests where asphodel and bog-myrtle grow.

Life for the crofters in Skye is not easy. Emigration has drained off a measure of the good old stock; fishing has been all but ruined by the incursion of trawlers into coastal waters; sheep-farming has failed; potato-growing has failed; the people, used to little and not expecting much, will not labour greatly to make sour land sweet, and little land is cultivated except in Sleat.

All the year round there is the work of the farm and the crofts and a little fishing, although trawling has spoilt the old abundance; hay has to be scythed—just enough on a croft to feed your cow through the winter; vegetables must be dug and the cattle herded. In autumn the golden fields look strangely diminutive and very homely lying at the foot of the Cuillins. Corn, growing almost down to the shore in this fertile valley-mouth, must be cut and dried, if only the north wind will blow, freeing the island from the southerly clouds and rain.

(iv)

"The natives have cows, sheep, barley and oats and live a harmless life being perfectly ignorant of most of the vices which abound in the world. They know nothing of money or gold, having no occasion for either; they covet no wealth, being fully satisfied with food and raiment; they have an agreable, hospitable temper for all strangers; they concern not themselves about the rest of mankind, except the inhabitants of the north part of Lewis. They take their surname from the colour of the sky, rainbow and clouds."

So wrote Mr. Martin Martin in his *Account of the Hebrides*, published in 1703, about the inhabitants of Harris, the southern smaller and more hilly part of the island of Lewis and Harris. It was this book which gave Dr. Johnson, in his early youth, the desire to visit the Hebrides, a desire which he realised in his sixty-fourth year, that was in 1773, in company with Boswell.

Johnson and Boswell did not visit the island of Lewis and Harris, but only Skye, Coll and some of the smaller islands of the inner Hebrides. Their sea-travelling was decidedly adventurous, in particular their journey from Skye to Coll. Even to-day the mail steamer from Tobermory to this island sometimes has to abandon landing her passengers. On land in Skye they fared easily and, welcomed as guests everywhere, certainly experienced the hospitable temper of the islanders. Whether or not the inhabitants of Skye and the neighbouring islands coveted wealth it is impossible to say, but they certainly needed money to pay their rents. The islands were in fact losing a large proportion of their population on this account. When in 1762 a ship sailed from Portree to America full of emigrants "the people on shore" (Boswell's words) "were almost distracted when they saw their relatives go off: they lay down on the ground, tumbled and tore the grass with their teeth. This year there was not a tear shed. The people on shore seemed to think they would soon follow. This indifference is a moral sign for the country."

In Lewis and Harris, at the time of Johnson's visit to the Hebrides, the population was, mainly owing to the kelp industry and to the improvement in potato cultivation, beginning to increase steadily. Between 1755 and 1830, the population increased from 12,500 to nearly 30,000. To-day, over a hundred years later, the population is a little over 33,000, of whom about 5000 live in the capital, fishing port and marketing centre of Stornoway, and about 5000 in the small villages in the extreme north of the island around Ness.

The island is in effect an immense peat bog, couched upon the granite with conical-shaped hills rising to about two thousand feet to the north of the narrow isthmus which connects South Harris with the rest of the island. There are a few isolated and gradually rising hills in the middle and northern part of the island. The villages or collections of crofts are all located along the coasts of the island, where alone there is sufficient grazing for cows and sheep. And sufficiency of grazing is a relative term, for the inhabitants of the island of Bernera on the West Coast send their sheep in the summer forty miles out to the Flannan Islands, where the sheep are landed in ships, for grazing. It is certainly grazing land which will determine the future population of the island.

Owing to the crofting legislation of the past fifty years, the idyllic economic state of the islanders which Mr. Martin described is being in part realised. The crofter family are unfortunately obliged to make contact with most of the vices which abound in the world until such time as one of them inherits the croft and has gathered sufficient wealth to pay the small (and invariable) land rent and to supply himself with such necessities as tea, sugar and oil for the rest of his life. He will also have to be able to buy his oatmeal, for although oats are the main and almost its only cereal crop grown on the long narrow crofts, the land has so deteriorated in quality that the oats must be used for cows, sheep and hens and not for porridge and cakes. It is true also that a few of the crofter's sons may become weavers of the celebrated Harris tweed and so stay at home: but they must perforce learn a few of the world's vices in dealing with the Stornoway cloth merchants.

Unquestionably, however, were it possible to utilise a larger amount of land, the population would increase rapidly, for employment in Glasgow, in the civil engineering works of the north of England and, above all, in the U.S.A. and Canada is not so easily come by in these days. The work of the model farm on Arnish moor is in this connection of exceptional importance. Successful experiments have been conducted in clearing land of peat, in growing turnips (potatoes and beetroot are the only root crops grown by the crofters) and in improving the quality of livestock. This farm has been waging a gradually successful battle against the tubercular cow and has greatly increased the milk yield of the island.

The first of the two most decided changes which have

come over the island in the past fifty years is the building of
the new stone houses in place of the old "black" houses.
These latter, which have rarely been pulled down and still
are used for sheep and hens, are constructed with stone walls
about three to four feet high, continued with peat and loose
stones and a peat roof, and are called "black" houses because
of their absence of windows. The new houses are well-built
square structures of stone. A great deal of home-made re-
inforced concrete (the iron from the hubs of cart-wheels
supplying the reinforcement) is used for lintels, window-
frames and small subsidiary buildings such as sheep-houses.
The building is particularly good in villages such as Barvas
and Port of Ness. In this northern part the inhabitants are
clearly of Scandinavian origin, and their farming is superior
to that of the rest of the island. It is only here, too, that
barley is grown.

The second change is the creation of a road system which,
however inadequate, links Stornoway with Tarbert and
South Harris, with villages on the western coast such as
Uig, Callanish and Carloway, and with Ness. Practically
every village of any size in the island has two buses which
ensure the carrying of all goods and passengers from Stornoway. The task of the driver of these buses is as onerous as
it is important. The surfacing of most of the roads is extremely bad, and the wear and tear on the vehicles is very
great. The Hebrideans, like the Italians, take naturally to the
motor-car, and in a similar spirit. The result of this road
system is the centralising of the island's economy upon
Stornoway and the decay of ports such as Ness and Tarbert.
The former, which was at all times a dangerous port, is now
virtually disused.

A second result is the disappearance of the horse or pony
from the crofts—and the use of the iron from the cart-
wheels! Horses are still used in some of the southern islands
such as South Uist, although it is impossible to conceive
that a man to-day should see the sight described by Mr.
Martin Martin: "As I came from South Uist, I perceived
about sixty horsemen riding along the sands, directing
their course for the east sea; and being between me
and the sun they made a great figure upon the plain
sands."

Stornoway, which faces nearly due south on the junction
of the Eye peninsula, which juts out from the east coast of
Lewis almost due east, is built of grey stone, except for a

80   LOCHBOISDALE AND THE WATERY LANDSCAPE OF SOUTH UIST, OUTER HEBRIDES

81   THE MIGHTY CLIFFS OF BERNERAY, OUTER HEBRIDES

few recently constructed houses which are, surprisingly, of brick—and Belgian brick at that! The town contains a Victorian-Gothic castle, not, however, of the worst variety, which was bequeathed to the town by Lord Leverhulme. Behind the castle rises Lady Lever Park, which contains some fine trees, including, of course, a great number of mountain ash, and pleasant walks by the side of the fiercely running streams which empty themselves into Stornoway Harbour with great violence. Gulls and the smell of herring dominate the water-front of Stornoway, and the sight and smell are so vivid that one is inclined to be homesick for them after a stay of only a month on the island.

The island itself is little visited by tourists, except for a few who come in the summer and pass a day or two in Stornoway. The recently begun air-service will make little difference, for the villages are very inaccessible. The buses leave in the afternoon or evening from Stornoway. After a four to five hours' journey to Uig or Rodil, the visitor cannot be assured of finding more than a night's lodging offered him from pity of his homeless condition. The islanders are far from inhospitable, but the lack of space and the fact that "tourism" as an industry has not begun, makes the stay of a visitor who has neither introductions nor a very obvious willingness to fit himself in with the daily life of the croft an impossibility.

The scenery of the island is decidedly less dramatic than that of Skye. Only to the north of Tarbert in the hills of the Forest of Harris (and they are extremely difficult to reach) is there anything approaching the glens and gorges of the Western Highlands or the Cuillins. But the villages of the west coast have an attraction which can well outweigh, to the hardy lover of Nature, the more usual charms. Here on the small "fjords" which run inland from the Atlantic he will find villages of great melancholy beauty, such as Callanish with its Druidical stones, or Tolstageluish lying between the Atlantic and a small lake, from which rises a nearly vertical hillside. Here he will meet, too, with people very unlike the poetical half-wits of the west coast of Ireland. At least five men out of ten have either worked in America in the course of their youth or have travelled about the world in the Army or Navy. The life of the croft is not on that account disturbed with restlessness. There is far more real knowledge of the world and of the values which make life worth living to be found in Lewis and Harris than in any other part of Great

83   IN STRATH DON : Pooldhidie Bridge over the Don, Aberdeenshire

CHAPTER V

THE LOWER GRAMPIANS: DEESIDE, DONSIDE AND SPEYSIDE

My first yearning for Deeside and the lower Grampians came in a sordid, squalid, altogether horrible munition works at Coatbridge during the war. Every morning at six o'clock we would stumble blindly over a bridge beyond a pub with the sweet name of "The Bloom of(f) Aberfeldy," down into a whippet-haunted clump of houses and over a smelly waste to the workshops: every evening at 5.30 p.m. we would just as blindly return. The interval between gave a thorough taste of what Hell would be—a monotonous, dreary existence without hope. During the night-shift I could wander out at times into the yard and enjoy painfully the sharp-edged stars, but their splendour meant nothing beside the agony of sleepiness which invariably began at 2 a.m. and thinned off again at 4 a.m.

To this misery came a tall, straight, red-headed Aberdonian with a rare descriptive gift, enamoured of pigs and poultry. He would push aside the industrial horror round us and paint instead a marvellous screen of light and thrilling colour held over deep valleys and superb mountains. His voice, with its slight sing-song intonation, would take up one magnificence after another and make all of them heartrending to us who desired something more of life than prostitution to a shell.

Magic names all of them: Aboyne, Banchory, Kincardine O'Neil, Ballater, Braemar, Dinnet Moor, Morven, Hill of Fare, Glentanar, Bennachie, Kintore, Alford, Allargue, Kildrummy: invested with a human inspiration not far from tears, for we were very young at that time. I swore then, in an enthusiasm of trust, that I would make that pilgrimage—confident that the War would pass over me. Even at Montrose, in barracks, when beyond that clear-aired, stormy, friendly town I could see the frail purple outlines of the hills and wander along a vast sandy shore, interrupted by great salmon traps, to the North Esk—and know that it came from the high hills. I felt that the Grampians were waiting for me, eternally patient and unswervingly kind. At that time everything had twice its glamour and twice its significance for the senses, conscious of death, they took an instant pleasure and held an eager memory.

Ten years later I returned—to find that old magic all but gone, and the pilgrimage up Deeside to the places of great moment and reminiscent splendour an unhappy con- templation of banality after banality. Banchory, Aboyne and Ballater could not be the places the Aberdonian described: something had gone from them even if one made allowances for the imagining of youth and that something held all the beauty and radiance of the world.

Later, when I had come to the presence of the Cairngorms and found a new world of experience and a wiser patience, I could be more tolerant towards the commercialism of Deeside and even enjoy, with a wry abandon, the professional slickness and the "bumptious" snobbery of the Highland games. I reached the point where even the gashed hillsides, whence the fine trees had been torn away and immolated in ugly sawmills, had a splendour and a sorrowful beauty of their own, and I could take out little vignettes of landscape frames in the shadows of the Cairngorms.

One is, unconsciously perhaps, unfair to Deeside, because Lochnagar has been besmirched in a poem of disgusting ban- ality and fashion-plate civilisation has been scattered over the villages and castles at its base—because royalty persists in its formalities in a land which lives for freedom and a wild inconsequence. But the consequences of fashion and popu- larity have brought Deeside and the lower Grampians into the dress specifications of the ladies' columns of the press—the discussion of what is most suitable for the opening of the season and district tartan which most effectively identifies a society hostess with a deer-haunted wilderness.

The great corries of Lochnagar are hidden behind the smug insincerity of obsequious officials staging a welcome to a royal personage, and the profusion of "obelisks, pyramids, tombs, statues, cairns and seats of inscribed granite" which was the gift of a Victorian favour to a landscape where it could only appear paltry and almost obscene, brought to the bareness of everlasting hills the frumpery of an Albert Memorial.

84   THE DEE VALLEY AT INVERCAULD, ABERDEENSHIRE

THE BROAD REACHES OF THE LOWER DEE, NEAR ABERDEEN

Yet the Highlands were beloved, as Lytton Strachey shows in his *Queen Victoria*:

> " 'Oh! What can equal the beauties of nature!' she exclaimed in her journal, during one of these visits. 'What enjoyment there is in them! Albert enjoys it so much; he is in ecstasies here.' 'Albert said,' she noted next day, 'that the chief beauty of mountain scenery consists in its frequent changes. We came home at six o'clock.' "

Deeside lives in the shadow of Lochnagar, even if in the middle reaches of the Dee the outliers of the Cairngorms make their own contribution to landscape beauty and the high peaks rise in a continuous wall beyond Braemar.

The conventional view of Lochnagar behind that peculiarly ugly nineteenth-century erection, Balmoral Castle, is perpetuated by millions of postcards, but Lochnagar ought to be enjoyed from other and better viewpoints. There is the famous view from the old bridge at Invercauld, where the Dee rushes broadly beneath and the terraces of the Ballochbuie Forest rise in magnificent gradations of form and colour to end in the noblest terrace of all, described by the corries of Lochnagar. This view is at its best in the late autumn, when the colours are at their strongest and the sky a cloudless turquoise.

Better still is the panorama from Craig Leek, a prominence immediately behind Invercauld House. From this miniature mountain, which is less than two thousand feet high, pushed forward into the valley with the Dee swelling in a semicircle round it, one can look over the finest part of Deeside, beyond Braemar to the west and to Balmoral in the east, but its most impressive view lies to the south, beyond the valley of the river itself, its forests now only a dark green foreground throwing into prominence the great folds and buttresses which swell up to a conclusion in a single rounded peak, the summit of Lochnagar. No corries are visible here, only the cairn on a semicircle of rock crowning a symmetrical landscape.

The third view comes at the end of a mountain walk over the peaks which stretch in a series of abrupt switchbacks to the east of the Clunie Water and Glen Callater. One can stand at the edge of the deep valley beside Loch Phadraig, a small blue gem, set in a narrow pass between steep hills, and look down on the deer crossing in hundreds the waste

of Ballochbuie Forest and across a wide uneven barrier of
grey stone, interrupted only by heather which sweeps up
to a wilderness of rock with no definition, either of corrie
or peak, to relieve its insignificant immensity. That ridge
walk is one of the finest short expeditions from Braemar as
it discovers magnificent pictures of the distant Cairngorms,
long perspectives down the Dee Valley, and at the same time
opens up narrow glens and exquisite little corners of forest.

On the west side of Glen Clunie one can make the conventional climb to the top of Morrone and wander over a deeply
heathered moorland with few declivities, as far as Sgor Mor
and An Socach. At this last and highest peak, which barely
projects above an almost featureless brown plateau, one can
look across to Loch Vrotachan, with serrated peaks to the
west of the Devil's Elbow, or south-west to the closely set
quartet of hills cutting the skyline beyond Loch nan Eun
and reaching their highest point at Glas Tulaichean. Those
are the hills which, with Beinn a' Ghlo, overlook the road
from White Bridge to Blair Atholl through Glen Tilt. The
whole country, as seen from the far end of the shoulder of
Socach, with the peak of Beinn a' Ghlo giving symmetry and
definition, is one of the wildest in the Grampians and is best
enjoyed, like Lochnagar, from a distance. From An Socach
one can clamber down the hillside over occasional narrow
terraces of rock to the Baddoch Burn and thence to Braemar.

Parallel to the Glen Shee road, and completing the series
of great glens running down into Forfar, Glen Isla has some
very fine features. Lintrathen Loch, although it lies among
the foothills, has a restrained dignity and fine beauty of its
own. Seen from Creigh Hill, it defines and clarifies the immense perspective of rich country bounded by the rolling
uplands which stretch from the outskirts of Perth almost to
Forfar, reaching their highest point at Auchterhouse Hill.
With that vision of green and silver in front of one's eyes,
one goes up the river Isla, along a road which rises very
rapidly and becomes more and more narrowly enclosed as
the hills gather themselves for the last movement upwards
to the great plateau at the end of the glen.

To the east and west, individual peaks rise in enormous
symmetrical progression, becoming steadily higher until they
sweep up to the lofty wall topped by Glas Maol, a mountain
which dominates Glen Isla on the one side and the Devil's
Elbow on the Glen Shee road on the other. Up to this point
Glen Isla does not present the constant regular slopes which

one finds at Glen Clova and the landscape is, on the whole, wilder because the steepness of the ascent is greater. At the very top, to the east, the steep slopes rise to a flat tableland which stretches across to the upper waters of Glen Doll and sweeps round the valley of the South Esk to Loch Muick.

The whole of this country is wild in the extreme, but its quality is one of gloomy atmosphere and desolation beneath overweighted skies: it emphasises those peaks which rise out of it from Broad Cairn across to Tolmount at the end of Glen Callater: Carn an Tuirc, Glas Maol and Creag Leacach. The impression one has of this plateau at the end of Glen Callater, with its terrific crescent of steep slopes, is intensified when one comes close to the high precipices and almost perpendicular walls which come together under the top of Glas Maol. Of this whole series the finest is undoubtedly Creag Leacach, which rises in a steep narrow ridge from which one can look over the immense world of peaks gathered round Glen Shee.

(ii)

To the collector of peaks ranging above three thousand feet or the irrepressible mountaineer looking for steep corries and frowning cliffs, the pleasant uplands surrounding Glen Esk or the great rolling moors which sweep down on County Angus are so unattractive and so little productive of exciting rewards that he would neglect them and pay tribute to more imposing panorama elsewhere.

Yet if I were asked to describe any area which, in retrospect, had a finer nostalgic quality and a deeper feeling of harmonious beauty and underlying peace, I could not do otherwise than choose the land lying between Esk and Clova, with its uncertain extensions north into Deeside. The line of the Grampians rounds off and interprets a fine pastoral landscape, and one may derive more intense delight from the small excellencies of this rich land—little glens and knolls, sparkling burns, secluded woody corners, miniature cliffs of earth and green deep meadows—and have a sensation of greater perspectives and intensities of colour.

County Angus and Forfar have always the suggestion of the Kailyard school—the influence of Kirriemuir and the early Barrie writings—but the smooth uplands, windswept and pure with an atmosphere so clear that the eyes are dazzled and the senses roused to a vigorous assertion of life, have their own power to cast aside such artifice and bring one back to origins and simple wonder of existence.

Two expeditions lasting each two days from Angus over to Deeside bring one closer to the real fineness of this country than any conventional journey over high peaks. The hillsides are dry and clean and covered with grass, except at the very tops, which break into a confusion of dry peat-hags; they slope down without abrupt declivities to the glens and sweep up again smoothly and evenly to a further wave of mountain, giving finally on the vast area surrounding the middle reaches of the river Dee.

The first expedition began at the railway station at Tanna-dice, went through Glen Ogil to the upper streams of the West Water River, thence to Tarfside, and beyond Tarfside through the Forest of Birse down to Aboyne.

Standing on the Hill of Garbet, at the end of a footpath which begins on the brilliant brown flats of Glen Ogil and disappears almost at once in the heather, one can look over miles of plain stretching in a perfect gradation of colour beyond the long curves of the foothills, until the solitary lighthouse on the Usan coast beyond Montrose cuts across the horizontal planes and points a fine white pencil against the dazzling radiance of light held in the sea.

There is no part of that picture which is prominent enough to be caught by a camera or be simplified to a few well-defined features such as one can enjoy in the pictures of D. Y. Cameron. It is an intricate succession of fine lines and thin shadows, almost lost in light, giving an impression of space which is beyond definition.

As one goes over the first range of hills, over the top of Betty Wharran, impeded by slippery grass and blazing sun, one looks down to a shallow valley, with a river bringing a streak of white into the wall of purple, blue and green, the colours so well fitted together in an immense mosaic that it is difficult to decide where the hillsides dip into folds or swell up again to buttresses. The inequalities have been merged by atmosphere and by magnificent colour combinations into a flat pattern carefully designed to bring out the silver of the river and to emphasise the shadows and the white rolling surfaces of the clouds.

Now one begins to feel the attraction of the lower Grampians: an attraction of pattern and deceiving colour, seldom of desolate rocks and majestic corries.

The road to the glen through which the West Water runs,

86   ON THE RIVER DEVERON, NEAR HUNTLY, ABERDEENSHIRE

87   LOCH NA BO, MORAYSHIRE : Famed for its big trout

88   A GORGE OF THE ESK, AT GANNOCHY, ANGUS

89   THE AVON AT BALLINDALLOCH, BANFF-MORAY

goes down a stony and broken hillside to a high flat valley which runs past the steep bluffs of two well-defined hills and comes down beyond a clear, sheep-haunted stream to a well-built road beyond a solitary hunting lodge, and the landscape assumes the appearance of a well-populated pastoral country.

One can accompany the West Water down into the plain to arrive ultimately at Edgehill, or strike across a tussocky field into a hillside deep in heather, with no defined track, and after some toil come to a cut between two plateaux of slimy peat glistening in the sun. Beyond this plateau, through which runs a clear road, one comes, in some extraordinary fashion, to a deeply indented watercourse and emerges over the brow on a wide, smooth hillside swelling down to Glen Esk with a long, semicircular range of mountains, all of much the same height, holding up the clouds in front, and the distant waters of Loch Lee, rain-slashed by a storm descending from the sharp defile of Glen Lee, and disappearing in the masses of clouds to the north-east.

The whole of the valley round Tarfside, with its little clumps of trees, quiet fields and flocks of sheep, looks so peaceful and so contented that one can regard it only as a continuation of the rich meadows of Angus, but the hills beyond are covered with blazing heather which lies here in masses of colour even more dazzling than on the slopes of the Forest of Glen Tana, giving on Deeside.

At Tarfside I spent a cool, midge-haunted night under thickly crowded pine trees where I could follow the slow, even change from a stormy sunset illuminated by purple, red and crimson clouds to a clear, cool, green sky still broken by thin clouds, until at last all commotion, colour and form disappeared in an unbroken blue and the stars were vivid in the sky.

In the calm morning I went up a cart-track on to the hillside beyond. The track continued along a high upland, swept by a cold sun, past isolated farmhouses, until it merged into another deer-stalker's path which led over the pass, flat and smooth in many places between large boulders, as far as a misty hillside where the sun had not yet warmed the haze away. Coming down farther under the mist, one found a gloriously fresh country traversed by the waters of Feugh, the hills sloping down to a broad plateau where cattle were grazing. On the bridge across the river one could look into the shallow stream and see trout darting between the stones.

To the west, beyond the Forest of Birse, one could see still armies of pines lining the road, which twisted into the Forest of Glen Tana. The road itself invited one by its windings and by its distant suggestion of forest to go down into Banchory, but a less obvious course was to strike up a steep hillside on to the shoulder of Lamawhillis and, after a short, strenuous climb, emerge on a flat hillside covered by small pines, with the whole of Deeside spread out like a map beneath.

The Forest of Glentana covered the many slopes to the west right down to the Dee, and isolated woods gave a dark shadow to what was predominantly a green and blue landscape. Beyond the Dee the Hill of Fare, under a bank of clouds, stood up in a purple silhouette which appeared almost black in the clear distant light. The sun lay on the southern slopes of Deeside and over the top of Lamawhillis, touching to a living flame the early autumn heather in full bloom.

The road to Aboyne, after the soft hillsides, was hard and unexciting, although it passed through a dense, cool wood out of reach of the sun, and one could stand on the bridge over the Dee enjoying for the first time the sweep and rush of a great river. From the top of the Hill of Fare one can obtain the most exact panorama extending almost to Aberdeen, but the connoisseur of colour and light and shade can do no better than to wade through the heather on the low slopes of Glen Tana, the landscape rising slowly in all its magnificence of light around him.

The second journey had an entirely different character. It depended less on colour than the first, and it had no bucolic or pastoral suggestion beyond the storm-haunted, difficult clearings of Glen Clova. One can go to Milton of Clova by bus and thus avoid a few miles of walking along a hard road by the South Esk, which is in some ways a much finer river than the North Esk. The former, like the river Avon, is continuously and magnificently beautiful. Even when it goes through flat meadows, it winds gracefully as if it were deliberately stretching out a curving mirror to reflect the clouds and the distant masses of the hills. From time to time one passes fishermen standing there as patiently as statues, living in an optimism which is more easily inspired by a river of this quality than even along Deeside.

At the beginning of Glen Clova, just beyond Cortachy Castle, the hills come steeply parallel to the course of the river, forests crowding their lower slopes and pale-grey, stone-strewn uplands lying above, and force it into a defile, so that one goes higher and higher above the stream and looks down through narrow perspectives into the plain of Angus beneath.

Once beyond this defile, which lasts for some miles, the valley opens out and the hills to the west fold down to a high plateau before rising again to a ridge which culminates at the head of the glen in the two solid peaks of Driesh and Mayar. Just where the glen turns north-west the birch trees crowd more densely on the water and strain the sunlight to a filtered shadow under cool moss and grey stone.

From time to time one emerges from the woods and sees the hills on either side and in the distance, grouped symmetrically round a valley with Milton of Clova in the middle of it. The mountains to the north-east file up past the two lonely lochs, Loch Wharrel and Loch Brandy, to desolate marshy uplands which stretch in a semicircle round the top of Glen Lee. As one approaches Glen Doll, the contours to the north-east come closer and closer together until an almost perpendicular wall, hundreds of feet high, darkens the path; at Braedownie, a peaceful, pine-shadowed corner, one sees the bluffs of Craig Mellon rising sheer into the sky, gloomy and uncompromising, and up the glen to the north, where the early waters of the Esk come tumbling down, an impressive gathering of rocky scree towers up through heather-hidden terraces and forms a powerful landscape almost as formidable in its suggestion of power held at bay as the mass of Lochnagar, shouldering the clouds beyond the desolate moorland east of Loch Muick.

The road goes to the right up a steep hillside where the passage of centuries has worn it almost to a ditch, and after a time comes out on one of the most impressive wildernesses in the whole of Scotland. One has only to traverse this narrow path at sunset, when storm-clouds gather over the black shadow of Lochnagar and the mist drifts threateningly over the hills from the east, across the watershed which gives life to the North and South Esk and the river Muick, to feel how transient is the passage of one solitary in a world where eternity is an ever-present desolation.

This path goes on for miles through what is almost continuous bog, black and gloomy, with here and there, where an occasional narrow glen breaks it, a suggestion of richer colour. Turning at last towards the west one can look down from the hill, past a small hunting-lodge, to the dark water

N

of Loch Muick, into which pours eerily the waters of rust-red streams. Opposite rise sheer cliffs beneath the lofty plateau of Lochnagar.

In the broad light of day, Loch Muick has all the beauty of a large Highland lake, without the suggestion of strength and power which one finds at Loch Avon. In the simplifying light of dusk it grows remote and repellent in its suggestion of terrific forces beyond human understanding.

Down the glen one passes a few miserable houses, crosses the river by an uncertain bridge and enters the pine forest which lies at the foot of Lochnagar. That night I spent high up on the slopes of the hill to avoid the midges which are here a curse, under a sky swept clear of clouds and magnificent with sparkling stars. As the night went on I could see them emerging with changing lights which became more intense as the wind dropped down to silence and the birch twigs were immobilised in an exquisite pattern holding the stars under the screen of the sky. Towards morning a small group of deer came along the hilltop and disappeared again into the shadows without a sound.

In the early morning the mist came down suddenly, blotting out everything; it became cold and dreary, but I had to continue up the hillside in an ever-increasing obscurity and clammy silence, broken by the weird clatter of partridges and the alarming cry of ptarmigan. Instead of relieving the monotony, those cries intensified it; the gobbling sounds were in harmony with the obscurity and clinging mist.

The path which held on up the hillside, up a long and invisible glen, came to a cross-roads in the midst of an army of boulders. By taking the north or right path, skirting the slopes of Conachcraig, one could descend Glen Gelder to Balmoral by an easy route, trodden in the past by Queen Victoria and her attendants. To do so would have implied discouragement, and so the less distinct path to the west was taken which soon became involved in boulders rising one after the other in a confusion made less imposing by the simplifying mist. The strain of climbing was relieved by the closing-in of perspective and lack of visibility, since all I could see was a small circle of grey granite stones.

After what seemed a very short time, the ground flattened out and I was on the plateau between Meikle Pap to the north and Cuidhe Crom—the map at least gave that informa-tion; but all I had before my eyes was a pale-grey wall, with a slight drift of light overhead and the knowledge that unless one were careful, one might easily go too far to the right at much too close quarters to the great Corrie of Lochnagar.

At one point a stag appeared in the shadows, drinking from a shallow pool, with no suspicion of any human near it; its startled flight was the last touch in a lonely silence.

The road now led clearly to the cairn at the real summit of Lochnagar, at Cac Carn Beag, set apparently in the centre of a limitless plateau of grey stone; then it turned sharply on itself and continued along the featureless wilderness of the White Mounth. As long as it remained on the plateau the road was fairly safe and one could not go far wrong, but as soon as the path dipped over the edge of it, it became a confusion of narrow tracks which might have been easy enough in clear daylight but were extremely difficult in the obscurity of the dense mist.

At one point the obscurity became so great that it was impossible to tell whether one were going down or up, but a slight movement in the mist caused by the wind coming up the side of the hill made it possible to get the direction right again, and so, feeling a way along a wet path in the heather, with soaking legs, one came at last out on the hillside above Loch Callater where the mist was less dense and one could see the shadowy outline of the whole loch carefully set in a grey sheet beneath. The path ended at last on a hard track six miles short of Braemar.

"White Mounth": that was my first experience of Lochnagar: romantic and entirely satisfying, even if one saw nothing of the mountain and ran the risk constantly of being lost in an inhospitable moorland. Strangely enough, I have never felt any desire to climb the mountain again, largely because I have always felt that Lochnagar is a mountain which must be enjoyed at a distance. Its terrific corries, etched out of the rock by thousands of years of erosion, provide good sport for rock-climbers.

The two journeys from Angus to Deeside, completely different in every respect, give an insight into the beauty and impressive strength of the lower Grampians which subsequent and more local expeditions do little to strengthen or weaken.

Deeside itself has become commercialised to such a degree that one can only pass through it as rapidly as possible, content with an occasional climb to a near hill, such as the table of Morven beyond Ballater and the Hill of Fare behind Banchory. One can stand at a bridge, as at Invercauld or the

Bridge of Feugh, and spend an afternoon watching the salmon leap and twist in the stream beneath.

The two Esks, the North Esk and the South Esk, are on the whole more attractive rivers. The North Esk at Gannochy goes through one of the most beautiful wooded defiles in the Highlands. The Dee is superior to all other Highland rivers, however, in its open reaches right in the heart of one of the most desolate and wildest parts of the Cairngorms, but its one-time fine forests and magnificent larches have been cut down or decimated, and Victorianism has converted what were once simple, beautiful little Highland villages into miserable hamlets dependent on neo-Gothic country houses.

A more conventional expedition leads one up the valley of the North Esk to Loch Lee, beyond Tarfside, then over the hills to Loch Wharral and down into Glen Clova; or one can go up Glen Doll to the west of Glen Clova and, after struggling over dreary, difficult and boggy uplands, arrive at the well-defined, steep hills overshadowing the Devil's Elbow and the Glen Shee road.

(iii)

From Deeside one can go to Donside through a whole series of passes. The first communication is from Crathie to north of the river Gairn, thence to Loch Builg and up the Builg to Inchrory at the bend of the Avon and then due east along an uncertain cart-track to Cock Bridge. There are few points on this road of any serious interest, and Loch Builg is a dull stretch of water with the near uplands veiling the majesty of Ben Avon.

From Dinnet a definite motor-road goes over to Strathdon and from that point onwards the communications between the two valleys are easy. The best way to approach Donside is not from Deeside at all, but from Tomintoul, and the best way to approach Tomintoul is to go up the river Avon from its junction with the Spey at Ballindalloch; or, more romantic still, from the Lairig an Laoigh Pass along the terrific gorges of the Ailnack.

My first expedition into Donside was along the latter, and it took exactly two days, since it was beyond human capacity to do the entire journey in one. I went along the Lairig an Laoigh from Nethybridge and left it just where it comes

90 IN GLEN CLOVA, ANGUS

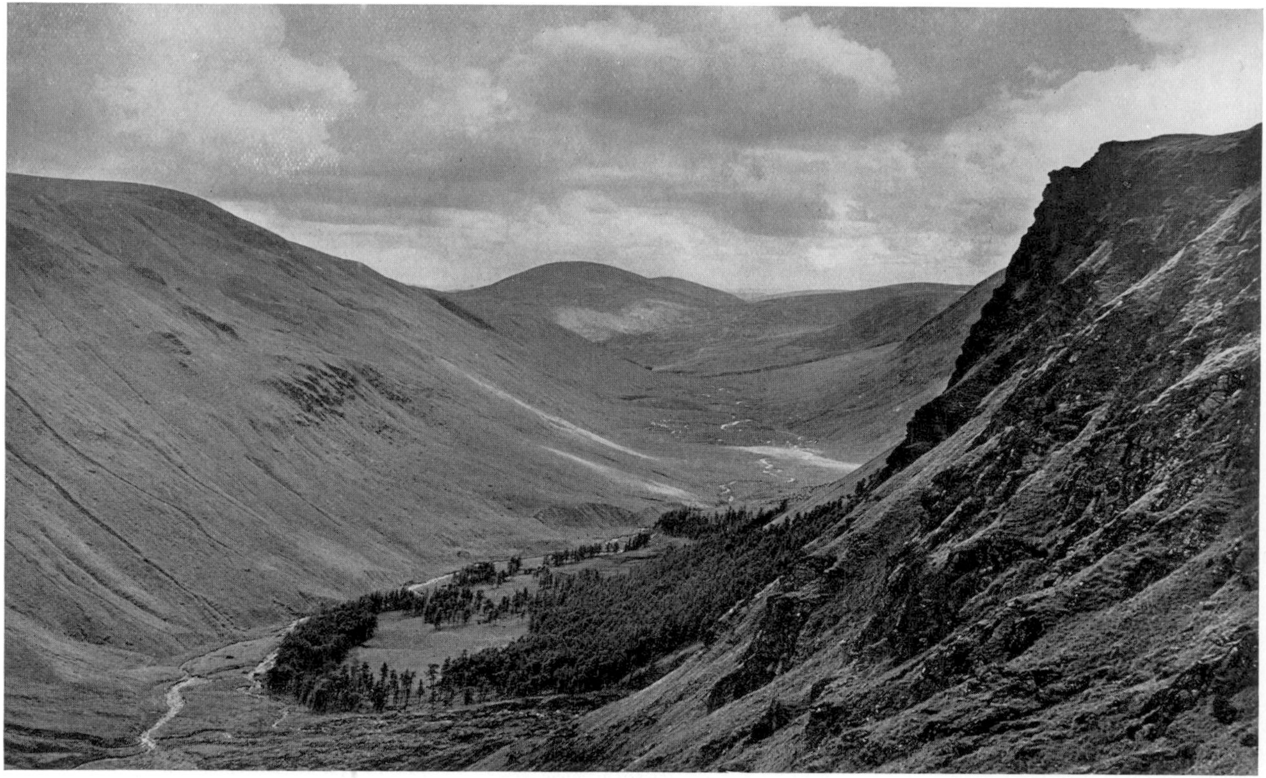

91 THE HEAD OF GLEN ISLA, ANGUS

abreast of Bynack More and dips down into the valley before
rising straight into the hill to meet the river Avon beyond.
One can, of course, go down to the Avon and walk along it
with a fair degree of comfort as far as Inchrory—one of the
most remarkable and imposing routes in the Cairngorms.
At the beginning there is a view of Loch Avon hidden deep
in the high hills, oozing through a narrow glen into the
clearest river, which, at the top of the road, is forced into a
narrow defile and after innumerable windings through an
irregular landscape—the foothills breaking in waves against
the high sides of Beinn a' Bhuird and retreating in confusion
before the slopes which guard the entrance to the wild corries
of the Slochd Mor—it becomes smoother and gentler and
the far hills merge into the pleasant green meadows bordering
on the Linn of Avon, a magnificent stretch of broken water
framed in birchwoods. I decided, however, to attempt the
much more difficult land of the Caiplich and the Ailnack,
largely because it was entirely unknown territory with its
own unknown difficulties.

On a day of sunshine, with no clouds and few shadows,
the moorland surrounding the Caiplich, with its solitary
shapeless peak of Geal Charn to the north, presents a monotony of shape and colour which is not altogether repellent.
It merely gives a suggestion of difficulty without reward.
But seen under a lowering sky, with rain threatening, it
becomes terrifying and unapproachable. When I got down to
the side of the river—because there is no footpath through
this region at all—the sun disappeared behind Ben Avon
and a slight rain began to fall. During the first few miles,
following a path made by fishermen and deer and rabbits,
there was only a thin trickle of mud over spongy moss and
tufted heather slopes: on the whole, not a pleasant experience.
At certain points the landscape opened out on damp meadows
at the side of the river, where the going was comparatively
pleasant, but the rain came down more and more deliberately,
until it obscured the distant hills with a grey veil, which
was only occasionally pierced by light.

After about six miles the river turned north-east and
entered its first series of gorges. One had to choose between
going over a thoroughly uninviting upland, which appeared
boggy and wet in the extreme, or sticking close to the river,
but at this point the cliffs came hard on the water which was
then in spate, and at "The Castle," where an absolutely perpendicular wall of rock rises up with much the same structure

as at Loch Avon, and the hills on the east side of the river present smooth dark slopes of scree, the only way through was actually in the middle of the stream. One had, therefore, to climb up a wall of scree about 70 feet high, depending on friction to maintain a hold, until one arrived at a precarious terrace rather more than 250 feet above the water. From this point one goes by a narrow deer-path along the face of what is little better than a cliff. At no time after that was it possible to get down to the river again, for the hills crowded closer and closer, so much so that at times it disappeared entirely from sight.

At one point, at the entrance to a glen to the north-west which cut at right angles to the river, one had to descend the steep bluffs to a flat meadow beside the river, expecting that after a short course round the low plateau of heather the water-side path would become possible again. At the junction of this glen the map shows a ford, but there was no ford that day, and so one could not avoid wading across and passing through to the Avon itself. Once more one could only climb up to the 2000-foot level and continue through a landscape which became wilder and wilder, reaching its highest point of magnificence just after the footpath, which leads from an isolated farm steading through badly drained and tussocky fields to Delnabo.

There was a constant temptation to leave that path and follow the river, since it had cut a canyon for itself hundreds of feet deep in what appeared to be rotten soil and scree. On the east side of the river the last slopes of the mountain came over in dark purple and blue masses, steeply graded, with hardly a flaw in their surface, until they broke over a narrow tongue of land between the Avon and the Ailnack, and disappeared in pine forests. The road to Delnabo ended on a precarious ridge of broken soil pitching steeply down to the river on one side and down to a narrow glen on the other, then went through an old plantation, past a hunting box and through a confusion of roads, over a bridge and up a singularly tiring hill, and finally dipped down into Tomintoul.

This journey which covers no more than twelve miles, took exactly eight hours, an indication not so much of its interest as of its appalling difficulty, a difficulty always romantic and menacing at the same time.

Tomintoul is a lonely Highland village with good hotels —a characteristic it has in common with most of the Speyside

and Donside towns and villages—but it is somewhat remote
from the more spectacular mountain peaks. It gives, however,
just outside the town, one of the great pictures of the Highlands: that of the river Avon, broken up into islands, going
through a wide curve into the defiles of the distant Cairngorms.

From Tomintoul down to Allargue and Donside one can
follow the Lecht road, which goes through quiet pastoral
landscape, along the Conglass Water, which is fairly inten-
sively cultivated, the moorland swelling slowly on either side
until the mountains come close on it near the Well of the
Lecht. Here a memorial stone has been erected to com-
memorate the building of the road by General Wade. From
this point onwards it climbs steeply along the side of the hill
above the water-course until it emerges on a gloomy upland,
the Warts on the top of Ben Avon just visible beyond a dark
intricacy of hills.

Standing at the top of the road, which reaches 2114 feet
in a comparatively short distance, one can see it snaking
through a landscape of a uniform purple and brown colour,
the monotony of which is impressive through sheer economy
of light, and have a feeling that the Don should run through
a wild and gloomy country with not a trace of cultivation.
But this impression disappears when one goes over the top
of the hill of Allargue and sees at the foot of the steep slope
the smooth forests and dazzling green meadows of one of
the richest pastoral valleys in Scotland.

At Allargue there is an inn notable for its cooking—a
good introduction to a valley which has a number of old-
fashioned inns, all of them good. From Corgarff to Alford
the Don Valley scarcely ever has an exciting moment. It is a
peculiarly well-bred, quiet, peaceful but interesting harmony
of woods and meadows and smooth upland; a landscape to
be enjoyed from a height, since it depends on pattern and
colour rather than on form.

And so, at Kildrummy, one should strike out for a long
easily rising slope, which comes to an end at Coiliochbhar
Hill, and reaches its highest point at an unnamed peak at
1747 feet. From Kildrummy, one goes over an old wooden
bridge, strikes off sharp to the east, along the side of a hill
fringed with beech trees, until one descends to an isolated
farm, long ago deserted, with the prospect either of going
down the hill for a short distance, followed by a steep climb
upwards, or of attempting a more gradual ascent on to the

shoulder of Craigie Beg, and thence up a singularly tiresome, long, even slope over a wilderness of cranberries, past shooting-butts and along an incredibly ancient bearded forest up to the very top, where one sees immense horizons to the east and north and south, the Don passing in a series of curves in a vast semicircle round the lower buttress of the hill.

The sky is the only limit of visibility at the top of this hill. The plain lies immense beneath, broken only by the symmetrical mass of Bennachie and its satellites. One has an ever-deepening impression of familiarity and experience intimately felt. Donside has, to one observer at least, a more profound appeal than the more extravagant glories of Deeside. Everything in it is smaller, more finely cut, more exquisitely finished; its colours are less strident and more delicately balanced. Standing on a hill and looking down on Alford and the grey plain of Aberdeenshire, the wind blowing lightly through the forest, which seems as old as the mountain itself, one can know, as nowhere else, the reality of eternal striving which lives in eternal peace.

(iv)

Of all the great rivers of Scotland, the Spey and the Avon are perhaps the most consistently beautiful, so much so that it is difficult to select any one part of their course and say that it is so supreme in its loveliness that no other part could be finer.

The Spey has its famous beauty spots, notably the view at Telford's Bridge, near Craigellachie, which has been the subject of innumerable paintings, but it is in its less accessible and more retired parts that it exercises its full force of attraction. From Newtonmore onwards it is, on the whole, a civilised river flowing rapidly, with occasional floods, when the waters turn brown and the islands are submerged, but the section from Loch Spey to Newtonmore is one of the most desolate, most imposing and most lonely stretches in the Highlands, and it gives no suggestion of the more luxurious magnificence to come.

In the low hills towards Aviemore, just beyond Kinrara, it comes sweeping round in rapid, wide curves, cutting away the sandy banks and making swirling reflections of the packed pine-woods growing beside it. Beyond Aviemore it comes into more open country, with wide perspectives and long,

92   IN GLEN SHEE, NEAR DALNAGLAR, ANGUS

93   THE BROAD SPEY, NEAR CRAIGELLACHIE, BANFF–MORAY

lean stretches of cloud hanging over it, but at Grantown-on-Spey, which is its second splendid moment, beyond the old bridge, it moves closely beside high headlands crowned by graceful trees, with occasional sallies of larches and delicate islands of birch and alder. One can stand on the high shore and look across to the distant Cairngorms and see under the sun this long curving ridge of beaten silver, alive and always fitting into the landscape as it moves beyond the birches and disappears into the distance.

Beyond the Cromdale station, one comes upon a further expanse of beautiful countryside, which comes to an end only at the bridge leading over the water to Advie station; here the road moves steadily up in a fresh green country crowned by scattered trees, until, at its highest point at Lettoch, it lays the complicated pattern of the Spey Valley between the opposing bastions of the Cromdale Hills and the outliers of the Monadliath Mountains, as far as Grantown, in a blaze of glorious colour and dazzling light.

Beyond that again, at Tulchan Lodge, where a sylvan glen, torn clean out of the hillside, rushes down under the bridge to the Spey, one can see the long line of the river moving like a snake beyond Straan Wood and the Hill of Dalnapol. Standing on the lower slopes of Dalnapol, in the early morning light when the sun lays long shadows and touches curving reaches of water to flame, one can enjoy, against the shadowy mass of Straan Wood, one of the finest pictorial compositions in the Highlands.

Perhaps the greatest moment of all comes when one crosses Telford's Bridge from Craigellachie, climbs up the hill beyond Overtown and walks over a wide plateau to the farm at Wester Elchies, and then through an ancient wood of magnificent full-grown oaks, beeches and ashes, held in a solid wall above the river, to Carron station. The wood at Wester Elchies, with its great succession of views down to the river and over to Charleston of Aberlour, with the high hills culminating in Ben Rinnes in the background, must be one of the fine places of earth.

To complete the Spey scene, one should go beyond Craigellachie for about a mile and a half, along an extremely pleasant road, and climb to the top of Ben Aigan. From this point one can look over the northern plain through which the Spey describes an extraordinarily involved zigzag course, going as far as Lossiemouth to the north, and on a very clear day one can see the line of the coast as far round as Findochty. Almost at one's feet, in a green stretch of valley, under smooth, heather-covered hillsides, lies Rothes, but one must go right over the brow of the hill to the south, looking westwards down the Spey Valley, to see a remarkable combination of mountain and river landscape.

The river Avon, from its junction with the Spey at Ballindalloch, right up to its source—Loch Avon—must be enjoyed in detail. It has its magnificent occasions, as at Loch Avon and beneath Slochd Mor, and at the Linn of Avon at Delnabo, but its beauty is an accumulation of fine impressions, which are never interrupted by dreary desolation, monotonous hill slopes or the heavy uniformity of widespread bogs. It has its protection of trees edging broad fields, where in the late autumn the corn stooks form thin lanes of shadow, and the road up to South Bank from Ballindalloch is one slow exquisite enjoyment. There is nothing more pacifying than this lonely walk, past silent farmhouses, with the river visible only at intervals beyond wide stretches of cornfields and densely fringed islands of birches. The path is soft and smooth going through an uninterrupted avenue of high birches. At Kilnmaichlie one can leave the path for a minute, go through the yard of a prosperous farmhouse and gaze down the deeply wooded glen into a splendid composition of shining water and dark shadowy hills. A few yards beyond the farmhouse, the path enters into its last stretch of wood and becomes a narrow track through the fields.

The slopes of Ben Rinnes fall away to the east and a new headland comes bluffly forward to push aside Glen Avon and allow Glen Livet to come north into the main stream. The road, now a mere suggestion of a path, traverses a tumbled moor and reaches its highest point just beyond Dalrachie, where one can see the valley widening out beneath, before it swerves round the rocky projection which marks the entrance to the Burn of Lochy and Glen Brown.

The road comes down to the river through the marshy meadow, crosses it by a narrow bridge and merges in a macadamised track on the east side of the Avon. Beyond the Bridge of Avon, it rises fairly steeply up the hillside, swerves round a quarry, whence one can look down on the river moving away into the narrow defile beyond Delnabo, with Tomintoul throwing an uncertain line of chimneys across the plateau beyond this curving landscape. From Tomintoul one can return to Speyside by taking bus to Craigellachie.

The only other river flowing into the North Sea at the

Cromarty Firth is the Findhorn, which has much the same characteristics as the Avon, except that it passes through a more desolate landscape, with occasionally deeper and more rocky gorges and that its finest parts, from Tomaton, north-east of Drynachan Lodge, are less approachable. At only one point has it that fine combination of valley, meadow and hill, which gives to the Avon and the Spey their magnificence This group of five, the Findhorn, the Spey, the Avon, the Don and the Dee, all of them so different and so impressive, is probably unrivalled anywhere else in Europe. The five rivers give character and strength to wide tracts of mountain which might otherwise be dull and heavy. They have led back into the hills the industry and the wealth of a nature brought to fruitfulness by human effort.

CHAPTER VI

GLENCOE, RANNOCH AND THE
PERTHSHIRE HIGHLANDS

ABOUT half-way in his epic wanderings from the wilds of Mull through Morven and down to Allan Water and Queensferry, David Balfour rested for five days in a magnificent place which Robert Louis Stevenson describes with economy and great effect:

"Early as day comes in the beginning of July, it was still dark when we reached our destination, a cleft in the head of a great mountain, with a water running through the midst, and upon the one hand a shallow cave in a rock. Birches grew there in a thin, pretty wood, which a little farther on was changed into a wood of pines. The burn was full of trout; the wood of cushat doves; on the open side of the mountain beyond, whaups would be always whistling, and cuckoos were plentiful. From the mouth of the cleft we looked down upon a part of Mamore, and on the sea-loch that divides that country from Appin; and this from so great a height as made it my continual wonder and pleasure to sit and behold them.

The name of the cleft was the Heugh of Corrynakeigh; and although from its height being so near upon the sea, it was often beset with clouds, yet it was on the whole a pleasant place, and the five days we lived in it went happily."

One would expect just such a consummation of beauty as R. L. S. suggests, only to discover, after climbing to the top of the steep slopes of the Pap of Glencoe, a gaunt stretch of rock in place of the idyllic scenery immortalised by Stevenson. It takes some resolution to move down from the Pap itself and wander along the monotonous ridge of Aonach Eagach, down, at the far eastern end, to the main road about a mile north of Achtriochtan, where Glencoe is at its wildest and dreariest, the sensation of a vastness of cloud, sea and

94   THE HEAD OF GLEN ETIVE, seen from Kingshouse, above Glencoe

95   THE HEAD OF LOCH SHIEL AMONG THE GLENFINNAN HILLS

96   IN GLENCOE, ARGYLLSHIRE

hill brooding over deeply cut valleys increasing at every step along the ridge.

One goes into the glen with a memory of the massacre of 1692, expecting to see a desolate country, but the massacre really took place in a fertile pastoral country surrounded by high forests, with a placid river running through green meadows down to one of the least wild sea-lochs of the Highlands.

If one stands on the hillside above North Ballachulish and looks over the widespreading landscape with the gentle waters of Loch Leven in the centre and the sunny meadows at the entrance of Glencoe beyond, one can scarcely believe that Highland superstition and cruelty could have anything to do with such a place; one must choose one's position with great care if one is to discover all the gloom and heavy splendour which Horatio McCulloch gave to it in his famous painting. The Glencoe he showed then is rather different from the Glencoe which appears just beyond the village, and Glencoe House, surrounded by pines and oaks and ornamental trees, is placed in a mountain setting which is more reminiscent of a south European country than the storm-stressed battlements of the western hills. The mountain slopes come down almost smoothly to the edge of the glen just beyond the lake, they are spaced off in even succession until, in the Pass itself, they become evenly balanced on either side.

The finest view of the whole district is from the top of Beinn Vair, where one can see the Pap of Glencoe with the long line of Aonach Eagach sprawling out into Loch Leven, forcing it to the north to the edge of the Mamore Forest and Lochaber to carve out an opening for the river Coe on the east. But one has a slight feeling of disappointment because, although the great panorama spread out before one's eyes has remarkable harmonies of colour and deep atmospheric effects, it gives no sensation of high mountains and over-whelming precipices. Several artists have tried to heighten the gloom and deepen the swell of the hills in the McCulloch tradition, but Glencoe, despite their efforts, has not the strength or magnificence of Glenshiel, and the cutting out of the new road has not improved the landscape. If anything, it has rendered it more artificial and hackneyed; the poor architectural quality of its features stands out in contrast to the fine curves and masses of the hills. To this combination of mountain gloom and long-drawn-out symmetry of mass

o

and line Glencoe still owes its power of inspiration and even of intimidation.

Along its southern and finer side a series of mountain buttresses stretches in parallel lines from north-east to south-west, with glens between them. They swerve round beyond Glen Etive to the hills which form the Black Mount massif and lock up the western end of the Moor of Rannoch. This group of parallel mountains is in itself one of the most exciting mountain ranges in Scotland, not so much because of the views yielded by every path, since the mountains are too closely crowded together for deep perspectives, but because of the extraordinary variety of mountain forms: variety which verges here on the fantastic and the grotesque. The Buachaille Etives, particularly the Crowberry Ridge on Buachaille Etive Mor, offer one of the most difficult and steep rock-climbs in Britain; seen from the King's House Inn, seamed and torn into deep couloirs and precipices, they are as strange as one of the Dolomites.

The great group which lies south of Loch Achtriochtan, a serrated background to the more immediate buttresses of Aonach Dubh, has a wealth of steep corries and gashed walls with broken wings standing out like towers, such as one does not easily find outside of Skye. Bidean nam Bian rises to the highest point in the Glencoe hills and from it one can look over the comparatively flat ridge of Aonach Eagach, beyond Glencoe, to the distant corries of Ben Nevis. To the south one can see peaks of Ben Cruachan, beyond Ben Starav, the western outliers of the Black Mount range. To the extreme west is the maze of hills crowding the entrance to Loch Leven, the distant gloomy waters of Loch Linnhe and the flat hills of Ardgour.

"Mountain-girded—there Bendoran
    To Schiehallion calls aloud,
Beckons he to lone Ben Alder,
    He to Nevis crowned with cloud.

Cradled here old Highland rivers—
    Etive, Cona, regal Tay—
Like the shout of clans to battle,
    Down the gorges break away."

The Black Mount group, which is comparatively seldom visited, stretches in irregular series from north to south,

97 A HILLTOP PANORAMA FROM THE SUMMIT OF BIDEAN NAM BIAN, at the head of Glen Etive,
Argyllshire

98 LOCH LEVEN, from above Ballachulish Ferry

99   THE BLACK MOUNT IN WINTER : A view across Loch Tulla, Rannoch

100　THE SHARP RIDGE-LINE OF BEN A'AN (THE COBBLER),
ARGYLLSHIRE

101　WINTER IN RANNOCH

beyond the King's House Inn. They lie to the east of Glen
Etive and form a smoother counterpart of the Buachaille
Etives to the west. The smoothness of their sides and the
comparative simplicity of their arrangement makes them
appear less imposing than the Glencoe hills, although
they reach as high levels, Clach Leathad, being only
150 feet below the highest point of the Bidean nam
Bian ridge.

Neil Munro in *The New Road* brings the Black Mount
country clear to the eyes:

" The inn stood on a desert edge; behind up rose the scowling
mountains of Glen Coe, so high and steep that even heather
failed them, and their gullies sent down streams of stones
instead of foam. Eastward, where the inn-front looked, the
moor stretched flat and naked as a Sound; three days' march
from end to end they said were on it—all untracked and
desert-melancholy. Its nearer parts were green with boggy
grass, on which the cannoch tuft—the cotton-sedge—was
strewn like flakes of snow; distantly its hue was sombre—
grey like ashes, blackened here and there with holes of peat.
The end of it was lost in mist from which there jutted, like
a skerry of the sea, Schiehallion. God-forgotten, man-for-
sworn, wild Rannoch, with the birds above it screaming,
was, to Æneas, the oddest thing, the eeriest in nature, he
had ever seen. It charmed and it repelled him. He thought
no wonder that the tribes who dwelt beside it should be
wild, and envious of Lowland meadows. The very sight of
it, so bleak and monstrous, filled even him with feelings of
revolt against the snug and comfortable world.

Half a dozen times before the noon that day he walked
up to the brae from which the moor was widest seen, and
looked across it with uneasy breast, and drank, as one might
say, the spirit of the wilderness, so strange and so forlorn.
Once he ventured out on a bit of its surface, and he found
an inland sea had likely once been there, and latter, maybe,
in the morn of time, a forest, for its old red fir-roots, like the
ribs of cattle, stuck out from the slime of peat. One spot
only—far off to the east, a silver glimmer plumed with little
woody isles that seemed to float on air—relieved the dun
perspective's desolation, and Ninian told him that it was
Loch Ba, and gave it loud applause for fishing.

'I know every creek of that same loch,' said he, ' and every
wee bit ealan on it. It is alive with fish; it is the nursery of
Tummel and Tay—it is the mother of the floods; there is
for me no fonder place in great Breadalbane, and many a

day the ghost of me is standing there upon the shore, remembering, remembering.' "

The noblest picture of all is perhaps displayed from the
slopes above Druimliart, which are just high enough to bring
Loch Tulla, Loch Bà and Loch Laidon into vision and set
them in a complicated silver pattern in the high plateau of
the moor. Rannoch Muir lies so close to the heavens that
autumn clouds, sweeping over from the west like heavy
water-logged sacks, seem to crush it in their passage. No
sign of life is here, except perhaps a herd of deer, their skins
scarcely distinguishable from the fallow brown of the
autumn moor. On such a day Rannoch might well be
the midmost world from which, eastwards, beneath a
clear water-green sky not yet swamped in the impending
storm, one sees perfection revealed in the pyramid of
Schiehallion.

The finest part of the Black Mount is a long ridge skirting
a series of precipices from the almost perpendicular slopes
of Sron na Creise down to Clach Leathad, with views across
the expanse of the Moor of Rannoch to Loch Bà; then the
difficult upper section of the Coireach a Bà, a confused and
slippery, yet extraordinarily interesting area, with fine views
down into Loch Etive on the one side and Loch Bà on the
other; from here one can go up to the jutting plateau of
Aonach Mor and higher up to Stob Ghabhar, its granite
rocks throwing a crescent shadow over the little lake at the
bottom. From this point one can see a hazy purple shadow
beyond Loch Tulla on the lower slopes of Beinn Achaladair:
this is the Forest of Crannach, one of the oldest in Scotland.

The whole of this range is shown in its proper perspective
beyond the shores of Loch Tulla, a lake fringed with old
trees which are the remnants of the ancient Caledonian
Forest. The lake and the somewhat flat country round it
are a simple foreground to a long, high band of hills thrown
across the sky to the north, with the more distant ranges of
the Ben Starav group visible to the west.

Ben Starav, which closes the upper waters of the Kinglass,
and gives to Loch Etive its most impressive aspect, resembles
in its formation some of the Cluanie Hills. The summit ridge
is balanced by an equal number of buttresses, descending into
deep corries and smoothed over on the south side to deep
folds unbroken by precipices, but almost as perpendicular
as the corries farther north. Ben Starav is in one of the most

THE BROADENING EXPANSE OF LOCH LINNHE, near Kentallen, looking to Morven

103   LOCH AILORT, on the West Inverness-shire seaboard

104 LOCH PATTACK AND THE NORTHERN CORRIES OF BEN ALDER, PERTHSHIRE

105   WINTER IN LOCHABER, INVERNESS-SHIRE : The Leacan Pass and Loch Treig

inaccessible parts of the Western Highlands, it is separated from the rest of the Black Mount group by an island of mountains rising above the swampy ground surrounding Loch Dochard and coming to its highest point at the Stob Coir' an Albannich.

Ben Nevis, treated in a conventional fashion, may be dismissed in a few words of reluctant and uninformed praise; it suffers from the easy attentions of the multitudes who troop up its smooth flanks from Fort William and, greatly daring, debouch into Glen Nevis; it suffers almost as much from the expert rock-climbers who practise their steps on its perpendicular corries and play joyfully with snow-bitten precipices; it has fallen a victim latterly to commercialism, and its dignity has suffered from the passage through its vitals of a water-power duct and the ugly factories at its base. Yet Ben Nevis, the Aonachs, and its rivals in the Mamore Forest across Glen Nevis, dominate the north and west of Scotland. It is an influence and a presence rather than an individuality: its splendour remains as imprisoned as are the inner plateaux of the Cairngorms but, unlike them, it looks down on an ever-changing sea. Only the Atlantic with its vast range of light can support this cloudy tableland; it is as much an ocean mountain as Ben More in Mull, even if the latter stands sheer above the pillared cliffs and the basalt monoliths of a hard-cut shore.

From time to time artists have attempted to transfer to canvas an impression of its great mass, but the version which comes closest to it is a poster issued by the London, Midland and Scottish Railway Company some years ago: clear and strong sunset shadows outlining a monster brooding over a shadowy Fort William. Cecil Hunt, in an impression of mole grey and velvety green, gave the mountain a strange life of its own, remote and reserved, a block of colour under a thin sky. A more accessible picture is that painted by James Docherty in the Glasgow Gallery. There, the mountain rises, bending over a shoulder towards the centre of the picture, with the wild, rolling moorlands touched by the colours of autumn beyond a brown and broken river.

Seen across Loch Linnhe, from the entrance to Glen Scaddle, it imposes by its immense bulk, rising above the lower hills, and the closer one gets to Loch Linnhe, the higher it towers into the sky. A fine distant view can be gained near Spean Bridge, where the whole series of hills comprising

P

the Ben Nevis group is brought into a long line of varied peaks, culminating in a high mass shadowed against the sky. Farther distant views of surpassing quality can be obtained from any of the peaks which close up the glens running into Loch Linnhe, particularly from the top of Sgurr Dhomhnuill. There, the broad lake breaks up the landscape and carries the eye directly to the snow-covered peaks in the far distance. The path up Glen Nevis round to Loch Treig, with the peaks of Mamore Forest to the south, drawn up like a serrated ridge from the abrupt headlands of Sgurr a' Mhaim to Binein Mor and the satellites of Ben Nevis to the north, is still one of the finest walks in Scotland.

Coming up the first part of Glen Nevis one has an impression of walking straight into a high wall which has no gradation whatever. One may climb up what is a thoroughly disappointing hill, notable only for the persistency of its mists and clouds, and expect a panoramic reward at the end—no more; but if the sun breaks out over the rocks and colours up the north-east face, the sensation of everlasting splendour swells up. There are few finer things than the high wall of corries which forms the summit and which is seen best from the sharp ridged top of Carn Mor Dearg. The two Aonachs— Mor and Beag—more symmetrical and more obvious, appear to be higher on this account, while Carn Mor Dearg itself is a regular cone, with steep sides crusted with mist and glowing with mysterious light in the afterglow. From those high viewpoints, Mamore Forest swells across the purple distance in long waves, not unlike the mountains of Glen Affric as seen from Aonach air Chrith, and in the far distance the carefully balanced ridge of Bidean nam Bian stands out above the Glencoe Hills.

Loch Treig, overshadowed in the centre by Stob Coire Easain, is rather a dull lake, and one cannot get a long enough perspective on it short of climbing Chno Dearg on the east side, up the steep boulder-strewn slopes beyond the railway. Its only satisfying moment is at the end, when one can look up the glens to the west and catch a glimpse of the high peaks in the far distance. Ben Alder lies at the end of the long Loch Ericht, a flat-topped hill reflected in the calm water beside the shadows of alders and birches, and at the end of the range of hills which began at Ben Nevis—a marshy, tiring wilderness, looking across to the Moor of Rannoch and the lofty hills surrounding Glen Lyon.

106   SPRING SNOW ON BEN DORAIN, PERTHSHIRE

107   A GLIMPSE OF LOCH KATRINE, WITH BEN LOMOND BEYOND

108   LOOKING TO BEN CRUACHAN FROM BEN LUI : Spring Snows

109 THE EASTERN END OF LOCH TAY, PERTHSHIRE

THE HEAD OF GLEN LYON, PERTHSHIRE

If one goes west from Ben Nevis by the green shores of
Loch Eil, at right angles from Loch Linnhe, one comes to a
loch as long, but more desolate in its silence, than Loch
Ericht—Loch Shiel. Ben Alder dominates the former and
Ben Resipol the latter. Seen from the top of Sgurr
Dhomhnuill, it is a landscape shot through with the
silver of Loch Shiel; from its highest shoulder one can
measure the true magnificence of Ben Nevis, crowning
a world of peaks. Loch Shiel and Sunart are quiet and
serene; even in the darkest storm they wind, gleaming
snakes of immeasurable length, into a twilight that has no
limit, into a mystery of shade beyond the rarest subtlety
of colour.

Ben Vair is the last peak of the Glencoe group to the
west: a high series of sharp ridges coming to a crescent round
the entrance to Loch Leven, notable, not so much on its own
account, as for the magnificent views it gives over a disturbed
mountain region. Its two sharp peaks lead the eye naturally
back to Bidean nam Bian and the distant hills of the Black
Mount, and from the top one can see southwards the mass of
Ben Cruachan, with its eight peaks, a mountain which covers
an even greater expanse of country than Beinn a' Bhuird.
Seen from the shores of Loch Etive with its highest
points nearest the water, it is a symmetrical and rather
fine mountain, which barricades as with a high wall
what would otherwise have been a dull section of Loch
Awe.

Dalmally lies spread out in its wide green valley at the
foot of Glen Orchy, giving form and weight and a heavy
splendour to the series of high summits bordering Glen
Strae, from Ben Cruachan right up to Ben Suidhe, the mountains falling down from almost 3700 feet to 2000 feet in a
succession of steep and almost regular gradations. At Dalmally one enters the dull, green landscape of Glen Orchy's
"sad mountains," with Ben Lui raising its coarsely folded
shoulders beyond the railway, and at Tyndrum one comes
straight into the gloom of the high enclosed hills which
sweep in a crescent round Glen Lochy, and swell again
beyond Ben Douran into a long ridge, which looks down on
Loch Lyon and the immensely long and fatiguing Glen
Lyon itself.

All the mountains in this group are smooth grassy pro-
tuberances, with only occasionally a difficult section. S. P.
Mais dilates with enthusiasm on the beauty of Glen Lyon,

but one must have occasionally experienced some flagging
of the spirits in trudging up its endless miles in a landscape
so featureless as to be oppressive when, even on the wildest
days of storm, the cloudscapes are not varied enough to break
up the tedious monotony of smooth slopes and uniformly
coloured masses.

It is only when one moves along to Crianlarich, at the end
of Strath Fillan, that one comes fully in sight of a magnificent
mountain combination—Ben More and Stobinian. The view
from Stobinian is one of the finest. It dominates the Braes
of Balquhidder just beneath, gives a glimpse of the quiet,
beautiful Loch Lubnaig, and lays open the whole of the
Scottish Lowlands right up to Stirling. To the east the mountains above Lochearnhead block out the full view of this
pretty, unexciting lake, and the mountain island of Ben
Vorlich and Stuc a' Chroin rise in silhouette to break up the
haze of the distant lowland landscape stretching as far as
Perth. From the north-east shoulder of Stobinian one can
look down on the whole of Glen Dochart, along the wide
expanse of Loch Tay, with Ben Lawers to the north and the
shapeless mounds enclosing Glen Almond to the south-east.
Ben Lawers itself has the merit of giving beauty and distant
magnificence to Glen Lyon; its attendant mountains in that
perspective fall into a wild Highland composition made
significant by the heavy shadows and steep slopes and buttresses culminating in Ben Lawers itself. Carn Mairg, north
of Glen Lyon, its importance emphasised by the sharp peak
of Schiehallion, forms an imposing and well-balanced group
of colour.

The whole of this country round Loch Tay and Loch
Earn, Glen Almond and the Sma' Glen, Loch Lubnaig, the
Braes of Balquhidder and Glen Falloch, has been illustrated
by innumerable artists and glorified by innumerable descriptive writers. Ben Falloch and Ben More and the Braes of
Balquhidder were the special preserve of the Glasgow School
and their disciples; and the river Lochy, just above Killin,
has a long tradition of canvases with autumn tints and
flashing water, dazzling blue skies and solid purple mountain
(slopes which are now almost the prerogative of shortbread
manufacturers). It is difficult to add anything new to what
has been said about this country: some of it has certainly
been overpraised.

Loch Tay is not a particularly interesting loch, and the
river Tay itself only begins to be really beautiful when it is

III FEBRUARY IN THE TROSSACHS : Looking to Ben Venue

112   THE TROSSACHS : The Pass of Achray

met by the river Tummel, when it passes down its narrow glen and through arching hills to Dunkeld. The Trossachs with their accompaniments, Loch Katrine and Loch Vennachar and Loch Achray, dominated by Ben Ledi and Ben Venue, are a fine stretch of quiet, highly tinted landscape. They have been commercialised as no other part of Scotland, but taken on their merits, they do not even compare with Glen Lyon farther north, and they have none of the inspiring splendour of the great glens which run westward from Loch Ness and Loch Oich. This is not to say that they are not sufficiently beautiful; but their beauty has become conventional and perhaps rather wearisome. They provide models for regular "beauty" pictures of the type which used to fill postcard albums, and they are still too reminiscent of the golden harmonies of the early English schools of painting. Association is too close to the honied colours of Copley-Fielding and the herds of Highland cattle which were so much the preoccupation of fashionable artists at the beginning of this century.

The landscape of the Trossachs can be easily spoilt; it has certainly not been improved by the roads which have been built along Loch Katrine. Farther north, beyond Pitlochry and Dunkeld, right up to the Pass of Killiecrankie, there is a higher type of this same kind of landscape; despite the "poster" approaches to Pitlochry, the river Tummel and the river Garry have carved through the hills a magnificent series of mountain compositions, which depend less on colour than on form. Christine Orr chooses this country for her "Road":

"The Road it runs by Atholl and climbs the midmost
 brae
Where Killiecrankie crowns the pass with golden woods and
 gay;
There straight and clean 'twas levelled where the Garry runs
 below
By Wade's red-coated soldiery two hundred years ago.

The Road it strikes Dalwhinnie where the mountain tops are
 grey
And the snow lies in the corries from October until
 May;
Then down from bleak Ben Alder by Loch Ericht's windswept
 shore
It hastes by Dalnaspidal to the howes of Newtonmore."

Q

The finest parts of the Highlands are still the secret, secluded places, not within reach of trippers' excursions: they are in the Cairngorms, the Black Mount, the Glencoe Hills, the mountains of Ross, the lower Grampians and Lewis.

113   ARDVRECK CASTLE, on Loch Assynt, Wester Ross

114   EILEAN DONAN CASTLE, on Loch Duich, Wester Ross

115 FYVIE CASTLE, ABERDEENSHIRE

APPENDIX

MONTROSE'S CAMPAIGNS

On "a March morning, with the ash buds black in St. John's Gardens"[1] James Graham, Earl of Montrose, one time Covenanter and now defender of the Royal Standard, rode out of Oxford bound for Scotland. As he rode north, the Scottish army was marching south, across the Border, to join the forces of Parliament against Charles I. Civil war was in progress in England; the Royal headquarters were at Oxford, where trenches were dug at the back of Wadham and across St. Giles, and colleges were turned into courts of barracks; the year was 1644.

"It seemed," wrote Walter Scott, "as if Heaven had at this disastrous period an essential controversy with the Kingdom of Scotland." Heaven's especial controversy with Scotland was to continue for a full hundred years, and controversy was indeed the order of the day in the mid-seventeenth century.

The kingdoms of England and Scotland, although united under one crown, had not yet coalesced into one State. Each kingdom was, in turn, divided against itself: in England, Cromwellian civil war was in progress; and Montrose was to keep Scotland in arms for more than a year. There was no stable central authority either in the State or in the Church. Questions of dogma, polity and hierarchy split the Church in two, and with it the nation, clan and family; while on the temporal side the civil rights and privileges of the Crown and dynastical issues were being settled by the force of arms. The separate strands of so many divergent trends, conflicting tendencies and mutually contradictory political and religious movements form a more than usually complicated political pattern, and this explains, perhaps, why history has been so extraordinarily slow in bringing out the unimpassioned verdict, for which she is so justly famous, on men such as Montrose, whose names are inseparable from the great events of the seventeenth century, and why, after an interval of

[1] *Montrose*, by John Buchan.

close upon three hundred years, the judgment of posterity remains that of Cavalier and Roundhead, Royalist and Covenanter, loyal partisans all and Covenanters for the most part.

At Newcastle, which lay on his way to Scotland, the Commander of the Royal Army, the Marquis of Newcastle, supplied him with a hundred ill-mounted troopers and two small brass cannon as the army with which to raise Scotland for Charles. Some thousand Cumberland and Westmoreland militia joined him before he reached Carlisle, only to desert him again as soon as he had crossed the Border. So that although Dumfries, the first town of importance on the Scottish side, surrendered without opposition, he could neither hold it with the few men now left nor remain himself in the neighbourhood infested with Covenanting levies. Disguised as a groom to one of his officers and accompanied by another, he rode for four days, travelling mostly by night, until he reached the house of Patrick Graham of Inchbrackie, Tullibelton, situated mid-way between Perth and Dunkeld.

Summer was drawing to its close, and the autumn glow was already on the hills as he lay hiding in the hills above Tullibelton, yet he was no nearer his enterprise than when he rode out of Oxford in March. Here word at last reached him that Alasdair Macdonald, with 1600 Irishmen, had come out of Ireland. He set out on foot to walk the twenty miles separating him from Blair, the appointed meeting-place, but instead of the large and well-disciplined army promised by Antrim, a mob of ragged and ill-disciplined Irishmen greeted his eye. Nevertheless, this was at last the nucleus of an army with which to begin the Rebellion.

Three separate Covenanting armies stood in the field against Montrose; the largest, under Lord Elcho, lay near at hand at Perth; Lord Balfour of Burleigh was at Aberdeen, and the Duke of Argyll and his men were in the west. To engage Lord Elcho first, Montrose marched through Aberfeldy to the wide plain of Tippermuir. On this first field of battle the relative strength of the Covenanting and Rebel armies stood at three to one; Montrose had no artillery, and his cavalry consisted of the three emaciated horses which carried him and his two companions from Dumfries to Tullibelton. Yet, under the "mountain torrent" of the Highlanders' general charge, Lord Elcho's centre broke and fled to Perth; so swift and so complete was the victory that "one might have walked to Perth on the dead," says a contemporary record.

Lord Balfour of Burleigh, at Aberdeen, was his next objective. He marched through Coupar-Angus, crossed the upper waters of the Esk and came within two miles of Aberdeen. Lord Balfour of Burleigh had the better position, superior numbers and heavy guns; the battle lasted many hours, but finally his cavalry turned and fled to Aberdeen. The town, the intervening two miles and the original battlefield soon became indistinguishable from each other in the general massacre which followed. As "The Sack of Aberdeen," the event looms large and dark in the history of Scotland; of the many historical slaughters, it is not least famous or horrible of them.

From Aberdeen, Montrose took the north-westerly direction and marched to Kintore, then farther west to Kildrummy, across the hills to Rothiemurchus and thence south to the head of the Spey and Badenoch. At Badenoch he fell ill, and the rumour sped over the country that the King's Lieutenant was dead and the Rebellion at an end.

Meanwhile the third Covenanting army, under the Duke of Argyll, Montrose's most formidable enemy, marched to Perth, thence to Aberdeen, following close on Montrose's track.

On 4th October, Montrose started out on his second march, Argyll following him, step by step, at a distance of seven or eight days' march. By a rapid march Montrose crossed from Spey to Tay, from Tay to Don. From Don, fearing the approach of the Duke of Argyll, he struck north into the uplands of Buchan, and at Fyvie Castle was very nearly caught in a trap by Argyll, whom he believed to be not yet across the Grampians. As Fyvie Castle stood on boggy ground, and Argyll's forces outnumbered his in the proportion of five to one, Montrose retired to a low ridge of wooded hills on the eastern side of the castle. Under cover of darkness, the same night, he slipped between Argyll's hands, and led his army safely to Strathbogie. The Duke of Argyll, having missed his quarry at Fyvie, and confident that the campaign was over for the winter, retired south to Dunkeld and sent his cavalry into winter quarters. Between Montrose at Balveny and Argyll at Dunkeld lay Badenoch, made almost impassable by the autumn rains. In a single night Montrose traversed the twenty-four miles of this rough country at the time of the year when snow lay on the mountain tops, and descended upon Argyll at Dunkeld. Argyll fell back on Perth and then went to Edinburgh to reap what reward he could from the Estates.

The first campaign of Montrose was over. Within two and a half months he had defeated three Covenanting armies and marched twice with an army several thousands strong across central and north-eastern Scotland, making each time almost a full circle: Perth being the extreme point in the south, Aberdeen in the east, Fyvie Castle in the north and Blair Castle in the west.

With Montrose's second campaign, the theatre of action shifts to the Western Highlands, to the country lying between Inverness in the north and Iveraray in the south. In order to understand the nature of this campaign or to see the four Jacobite Rebellions in their true proportion and perspective, some knowledge is necessary of the Highlands as a social system and of the physical aspect of the country, which, during the course of many centuries, bred its own type of warrior and evolved specific methods of mountain warfare. The feudal system in Scotland, imperfectly grafted upon the older patriarchal structure of the clan, not only played an important part as a third factor in the four Jacobite Rebellions —a given set of political circumstances and the interplay of personal motives and ambitions being the other two factors— but not infrequently it dominated and overshadowed all other issues. As this is true of all the Jacobite Rebellions, and as the best illustration of it is found in the campaign of Viscount Dundee in the Rebellion of 1689, it is sufficient to say here that Montrose's second campaign was less a military campaign than a punitive expedition against the Clan Campbell, a predatory raid into the lands of his most hated and powerful enemy, a revengeful settling of feudal accounts with the head of the clan, the Duke of Argyll.

In the shortest and darkest days of December, Montrose set out from Blair Atholl and led his men through sodden heather, when it was not a quaking bog or a trackless morass, across the uplands of Badenoch, down both sides of Loch Tay, through Glen Dochart and Glen Orchy to the shores of Loch Awe. When news reached the Duke of Argyll that Montrose was advancing south from Loch Awe to Inveraray, and that the impossible feat was accomplished of crossing a country, the secret of which, it was confidently assumed, was known only to a few shepherds of the Clan Campbell—

116 WINTER IN ATHOLL

117   THE STATELY TAY, near Blair Atholl, looking to Ben Vrackie

118   THE MASS OF BEN NEVIS, seen from Corpach

and at the time of year when all landmarks and paths were obliterated under the winter covering of snow—the Duke of Argyll took a boat to his castle at Roseneath, on the Gare Loch.

Montrose occupied Inveraray, and for many weeks the Highlanders plundered, pillaged and harassed the neighbourhood, and when the army went back to the north shore of Loch Awe all that could not be taken away was set on fire. From Loch Awe, through the Pass of Brander, the army marched west to the narrows of Connell, crossed Loch Etive and by a rapid march through Appin, reached Kilcummin (Fort Augustus) at the end of January. At Fort Augustus, Montrose was threatened by a Covenanting army, 5000 strong, under Seaforth, at Inverness, and by the Duke of Argyll, who was now pursuing him from the south.

In order to deal with the stronger enemy first, Montrose undertook a flank march from Fort Augustus in order to intercept Argyll at Inverlochy. If the tales of ravage and destruction perpetrated by the Highlanders in Argyllshire could be easily paralleled elsewhere—and much better historical examples of how to spread ruin in a short space of time over a large tract of land could be found without much difficulty—it would probably be less easy to find another record of an army marching in mid-winter for forty-eight hours, without a mouthful, across a tangle of wildest mountains, such as surround Ben Nevis, and succeeding not only in getting safely across but in bringing with them a small troop of horse. From Fort Augustus the army of Montrose followed the rocky course of the river Tarf into the hills, crossed to Glen Turrit and then went down to Glen Roy. When Argyll's camp came into full view in the moonlight, the army lay down, cold, supperless, and not daring to light fires, to get some rest during the night. In the morning, the Lowlanders, although outnumbering Montrose by a thousand, made no stand, and fled. Montrose marched north to Elgin, where Seaforth made his peace with him.

The Estates in Edinburgh, meanwhile, put the command of the forces in Scotland into the hands of two new men: General Baillie, an old and wary professional soldier, and General Hurry, a good strategist. They further appointed a War Committee, composed of such men as Lord Elcho, Lord Balfour of Burleigh and the Duke of Argyll, now grown wise in defeat. A representative branch of the War Committee was sent to the front to keep close to the elbow of the Commander-in-Chief, and to override him with their superior decisions. It is to this leadership *en masse* that some, at least, of the defeats in the following campaigns are directly due.

The next campaign is a long-drawn-out trial of strength between Baillie, who tried to draw Montrose, and Montrose, who tried to pin Baillie to a decisive battle. From Elgin, Montrose proceeded by way of Aberdeen to Fettercairn, crossed the South Esk and finally pitched camp at Dunkeld. At Dunkeld most of the Highlanders disappeared into the hills; as the hot sun melts the snow in the spring, so the effect of this long and ineffective campaign was to thin the ranks of Montrose's army almost to the verge of disappearance. To hold together what remained of his army, Montrose made a diversion into Dundee, and as the tired, ragged, ill-shod men fell upon the plunder and on the ale and wine discovered in the city, Baillie and Hurry approached within a mile of the West Port of Dundee. Montrose was now called upon to accomplish something no other general in Europe, it was said, could have achieved with equal success: to beat his men off their plunder and lead them, benumbed with the combined effect of wine and fatigue, at a rapid march into the safety of the hills. From Dundee, Montrose took the direction of Arbroath, and Baillie tried to wedge him between his army and the sea, but Montrose doubled on his tracks during the night and disappeared into the hills.

It is difficult to follow Montrose's movements in his next campaign; it is further complicated by the change in the relative position of the Highland clans on the Rebel and Royalist side. During the months from April to September, it was not once nor twice that he crossed the Dee, the Don and the Spey; for weeks he wasted Baillie's energy and tried his patience, leading and outmanœuvring him up and down the valley of the Spey. His first lightning march took him from Doune through Strathyre to Lochearnhead, and on through Glen Ogle to Loch Tay and across the shoulder of Schiehallion into Atholl; he followed then one of the Angus glens to Glen Muick, crossed the Dee and came to Skene. From Skene, partly to protect the Gordon country and partly to engage Hurry, who was operating in the north, he marched through the Upper Don, the Avon and the Spey. Hurry drew him farther and farther north until he reached the little village of Auldearn: here the attacker was for once attacked and taken by surprise. He displayed at Auldearn as great an understanding of the tactics of the defensive as that of the offensive. Warned at daybreak of the approach of Hurry by a chance going-off of an enemy gun, he made the disposition of the battle in a few moments: they were roughly a weak right, an almost non-existent centre of a thin line of Alasdair's men, and a concealed left wing of cavalry which was thrown into the battle at the last moment and carried all before it. The battle of Auldearn is memorable as a model on which the battle of Austerlitz was fought by Napoleon on a much grander and more spectacular scale.

Hurry's army was annihilated, but Baillie's was ravaging the Gordon lands and was now hastening southwards in pursuit of Montrose. At the Muir of Alford, near the Ford of Forbes, Baillie caught up with Montrose. Montrose took up a strong position on Gallows Hill, immediately south of the ford; as at Auldearn he concealed the greater number behind the crest of the hill; on the left rear he was protected by a marshy ravine. It was the intention of Montrose that Baillie should cross the river at the Boat of Forbes; Baillie walked into the trap and Montrose was able to carry out his plan of battle. As at Auldearn the Royalists suffered a crushing defeat and Baillie's army ceased to exist.

Montrose now gathered all available forces to make a final assault on the Lowlands. Crossing the Dee he marched to Fordoun in the Mearns, descended to Dunkeld, passed Tippermuir, crossed the Earn between Dupplin and Forteviot, down Glenfarg to Kinross. From Kinross he marched southwards, crossed the Forth at the Fords of Frew, passed Bannockburn, and on the 14th of August came within a mile of Kilsyth. Meanwhile the Estates put into the field two new armies, one under Lanark, the other under Baillie. At the battle of Kilsyth it was the Covenanting War Committee who gave orders and Baillie who carried them out. Convinced that the greatest calamity which could befall the Covenanters was to let Montrose slip out into the hills—of his defeat they did not doubt—the Covenanters, all unknown to themselves, first fell in with the calculations of Montrose and then, at the most inopportune moment, undertook a flank movement across Montrose's front. Montrose's victory at Kilsyth gave him the command of the whole of Scotland.

But, on the 13th of September, Montrose was utterly de-

R

feated at Philiphaugh. His army was surprised in the thick autumnal fog of the morning, the greater part of it, including the Irish, was massacred, and the remnant induced to surrender on a promise of quarter, which was never given.

The importance of Montrose in the seventeenth century is that he is one of a group of the earliest Constitutional Monarchists and Democrats: not what these two terms might connote to us in their old age, but in the meaning they could only have had at the time when they were emerging as definite political conceptions in the History of the Constitutional Law of this country.

He was one of the first to recognise the organic nature of the State and of the indivisibility of sovereign power, and to state his political philosophy in clear and precise terms. His declaration at Dumfries, "for the defence and maintenance of the true Protestant religion, his Majesty's just and sacred Authority, the fundamental laws and privileges of Parliament, the peace and freedom of the oppressed and enthralled subject," expresses his attitude to State and Church. He first came into conflict with Feudal Lords over the rights and property of the common people; in signing the Covenant he fought against the interference of the Crown with liberty of conscience of the Scottish nation; and, finally, taking up arms against the Covenanters, he was in revolt against the tyranny of the Kirk over the private life of the common man.

As a man of action, he had the gift of rapid decision and swift action of a great soldier. As a leader of men he could weld together the most heterogeneous elements and transform them into an efficient army; throw his men into battle by one word of command or encouragement, or lead them, half-dead with fatigue and sleeplessness, at a rapid march into safety, as at Dundee; beat them off their plunder and command obedience; accomplish feats of traversing in mid-winter Alpine heights with a full army and cavalry. A strategist and tactician, he was also an innovator and a reformer in the art of warfare.

From whatever angle we choose to view him, greatness could hardly be denied him. The full stature of the man is seen at the hour of execution: a great hush fell on the crowd as, sick and wearied out by long travel, he was led to the scaffold. At the supreme moment, as the hangman pushed him off the ladder, the hired rabble which came to pelt him with stones and execrations broke into sobs instead. After the execution the dismembered limbs of his body were exhibited in the chief towns of Scotland, and for eleven years his head stuck on a spike at the Tolbooth in Edinburgh.

INDEX OF PLACE-NAMES

(The numbers in italics refer to the *figure numbers* of illustrations)